A Critical Introduction to the Epistemology of Perception

BLOOMSBURY CRITICAL INTRODUCTIONS TO CONTEMPORARY EPISTEMOLOGY

Series Editor:

Stephen Hetherington, Professor of Philosophy,
The University of New South Wales, Australia

Editorial Board:

Claudio de Almeida, Pontifical Catholic University of Rio Grande do Sul, Brazil; Richard Fumerton, The University of Iowa, USA; John Greco, Saint Louis University, USA; Jonathan Kvanvig, Baylor University, USA; Ram Neta, University of North Carolina, Chapel Hill, USA; Duncan Pritchard, The University of Edinburgh, UK

Bloomsbury Critical Introductions to Contemporary Epistemology introduces and advances the central topics within one of the most dynamic areas of contemporary philosophy.

Each critical introduction provides a comprehensive survey to an important epistemic subject, covering the historical, methodological, and practical contexts and exploring the major approaches, theories, and debates. By clearly illustrating the changes to the ways human knowledge is being studied, each volume places an emphasis on the historical background and makes important connections between contemporary issues and the wider history of modern philosophy.

Designed for use on contemporary epistemology courses, the introductions are defined by a clarity of argument and equipped with easy-to-follow chapter summaries, annotated guides to reading, and glossaries to facilitate and encourage further study. This series is ideal for upper-level undergraduates and postgraduates wishing to stay informed of the thinkers, issues, and arguments shaping twenty-first century epistemology.

Titles in the series include:

A Critical Introduction to the Epistemology of Memory, Thomas D. Senor
A Critical Introduction to Knowledge-How, J. Adam Carter and Ted Poston
A Critical Introduction to Formal Epistemology, Darren Bradley
A Critical Introduction to Scientific Realism, Paul Dicken
A Critical Introduction to Skepticism, Allan Hazlett
A Critical Introduction to Testimony, Axel Gelfert

A Critical Introduction to the Epistemology of Perception

ALI HASAN

Bloomsbury Academic
An imprint of Bloomsbury Publishing Plc

B L O O M S B U R Y

LONDON · OXFORD · NEW YORK · NEW DELHI · SYDNEY

Bloomsbury Academic

An imprint of Bloomsbury Publishing Plc

50 Bedford Square
London
WC1B 3DP
UK

1385 Broadway
New York
NY 10018
USA

www.bloomsbury.com

BLOOMSBURY and the Diana logo are trademarks of Bloomsbury Publishing Plc

First published 2017

© Ali Hasan, 2017

British Library Cataloguing-in-Publication Data
A catalogue record for this book is available from the British Library.

ISBN: HB: 978-1-4725-3495-8
PB: 978-1-4725-2659-5
ePDF: 978-1-4725-3353-1
ePub: 978-1-4725-2657-1

Library of Congress Cataloging-in-Publication Data
Names: Hasan, Ali M., 1974-
Title: A critical introduction to the epistemology of perception / Ali Hasan.
Description: New York : Bloomsbury Academic, 2017. | Series: Bloomsbury critical introductions to contemporary epistemology ; 8 | Includes bibliographical references and index.
Identifiers: LCCN 2016038202| ISBN 9781472534958 (hb) | ISBN 9781472533531 (epdf)
Subjects: LCSH: Perception (Philosophy) | Knowledge, Theory of.
Classification: LCC B828.45 .H37 2017 | DDC 121/.34--dc23 LC record available at https://lccn.loc.gov/2016038202

Series: Bloomsbury Critical Introductions to Contemporary Epistemology

Cover design: Louise Dugdale
Cover image © Philip Habib/Gallerystock

Typeset by Fakenham Prepress Solutions, Fakenham, Norfolk NR21 8NN

For my father, Majed Hasan (1950–2011),
and my mother, Jamilla AlQaseer

Contents

Preface

This book offers an introduction to the epistemology of perception intended for students with some exposure to philosophy, but who may be unfamiliar with the epistemology of perception, or with metaphysical or epistemological debates in general. The book is heavily influenced by survey courses I have taught in epistemology, at various levels, and by upper-level courses focused on the epistemology of perception. I find in these contexts that the students benefit greatly from having both (i) accessible, relatively short but critical discussions of the relevant backgrounds, theories, central principles, and arguments, coupled with (ii) primary readings and articles. The book was written with this in mind, and so is best paired with readings for each chapter. Each chapter ends with some suggestions for further reading, and questions for reflection and discussion.

My intention is to present the material in an informative, clear and accessible manner, without too much technical detail. But I also wanted to provoke the reader, and for this reason I do not shy away from criticism and controversy, and from letting my own voice enter the text now and again, while leaving a number of dialectical or argumentative routes open for students to pursue on their own. Given the immense and growing size of the literature in the field and the many important and fascinating issues within it, I have had to be somewhat selective, both in terms of what theories and themes to focus on, and in terms of the particular arguments and objections to discuss. There are major, recurring themes throughout, and enough of an overall narrative and structure that the reader should, I hope, be able to see the forest and navigate a bit better through the trees.

The examination of debates in the epistemology of perception is preceded by an overview of (i) some background to epistemological and (to a lesser extent) metaphysical problems of perception in early modern philosophy (Chapters 1 and 2), (ii) theories of perceptual experience (Chapter 3), and (iii) some central questions and controversies in epistemology (Chapter 4). This prepares readers unfamiliar with the relevant history, key concepts, and related debates in epistemology and the philosophy of mind. More experienced readers can review parts of the background more selectively, depending on their needs and interests, and jump ahead to the chapters on contemporary theories in the epistemology of perception.

Each of the chapters on epistemological theories clarifies, motivates, and evaluates the theory, highlighting its answers to some of the following questions: Are perceptual beliefs justified, and if so, in virtue of what are they justified? Can the theory accommodate foundational beliefs about the external world? Does it capture the internalist intuition that a belief must depend for its justification on the subject's possession of or access to reasons in favor of its truth? Does it preserve the intuitive idea that epistemic justification is tightly connected to the truth? Does it provide a satisfactory response to the skeptical challenge, one that takes skepticism seriously without acceding to it? Each theory examined yields intuitive, positive answers to some of these questions, but has difficulty with others.

I would like to thank my family and friends, colleagues and students, who have helped make this book possible. I am grateful to my teachers at the University of Washington in Seattle, where I began to work on issues in the epistemology of perception as a graduate student, especially Larry BonJour, Ann Baker, Andrea Woody, and Bill Talbott; and to colleagues and students at the University of Iowa, with whom I have discussed many of the topics covered here—especially Richard Fumerton, who also provided helpful comments on an earlier draft. I would also like to thank Andrew Wardell and Colleen Coalter at Bloomsbury, and the series editor, Stephen Hetherington, for their encouragement and flexibility; and an anonymous reviewer for detailed comments and suggestions.

I am also grateful to Sarah McElligott for all her patience and support; to my children Leila, Elyas, and Jude, for being the best of distractions, and for providing lovely and vital time away from work. I would also like to thank Jennifer Kayle for providing me with much love and support when I most desperately needed it.

1

Skepticism and foundationalism in early modern philosophy

The chapter introduces the problem of skepticism through the work of Descartes, especially the central epistemological ideas and arguments developed in his *Meditations on First Philosophy*. We see how Descartes took introspection and reason to be the sources of foundational knowledge, and examine his attempt to defeat skepticism regarding the external world. We conclude that not only is the Cartesian attempt to secure knowledge of the external world seriously problematic, but that Hume's concerns deepen the skeptical problem, even challenging the claim that our external world beliefs are justified or rational.

Contemporary debates in the epistemology of perception have evolved from and in reaction to the work of the early modern philosophers, and so it is natural to begin our investigation with an overview of the early modern debate in the epistemology of perception. This is not meant to provide a comprehensive examination of that debate, but to present a helpful narrative, covering some of the main figures and their central arguments, with an eye toward its connection to the contemporary debates. We begin in this chapter with a discussion of skepticism and foundationalism in the work of Descartes, and turn in the next chapter to consider some influential attempts to respond to skepticism by Locke, Berkeley, and Reid.

Dreams, demons, and Descartes' epistemological project

We have all had the experience of changing our minds about something we once took to be obvious. Sometimes this happens because we become convinced that some apparent truth turns out to be false. I might realize, for example, that an oar half-submerged in water looks bent but is actually straight, or that the person approaching me from a distance looks like a friend but is in fact a stranger. And sometimes it happens because we are no longer convinced that we can tell whether what we once believed is true or false; rather than believe or disbelieve it, we withhold or suspend belief. I have come to be quite unsure, for example, of my ability to tell whether certain moral and religious claims I once believed are true or false, and so I have come to suspend judgment about them. When my confidence or trust in some particular belief or judgment is questioned, I might seek and offer further reasons in support of that belief. But if these further reasons are other propositions I believe or accept, I can raise the same question: what assurance do I have that *these* supporting beliefs are true? In this way I am led, quite naturally, to expand the class of beliefs considered until I finally ask a global question: Do I have any assurance, any good reasons at all, for thinking that any of my beliefs are even approximately true?

In his *Meditations on First Philosophy*, René Descartes (1596–1650) leads us in this natural way to wonder what assurance we may have for our beliefs. Since "a wise man never entirely trusts those who have once cheated him" (CSM II: 13),[1] Descartes attempts to scrutinize his beliefs and belief sources with the goal of determining which, if any, are trustworthy, so that he may have a stable "foundation" for knowledge. He proposes the *method of doubt* to discover whether there are any beliefs that can play this foundational role: if it is possible for a belief of mine to be false, then I should not trust it or accept it as knowledge; I must retain only what is invulnerable to this doubt— only what is *indubitable*.

Descartes was aware that many of his readers would be inclined to dismiss or contain the doubts raised above. We often change our minds about controversial matters in morality, politics, and science, but these are admittedly very complicated and difficult issues that deserve careful reflection, and surely not all truths are so difficult to discern. We do sometimes go wrong even in relying directly on sensory perception, as when we mistake a straight oar in water for a bent one, misclassify approaching vehicles in the fog, or objects and faces from afar or while drunk; but these seem to be relatively rare, or at least non-ideal, conditions for observation. In ordinary or at least ideal observational or perceptual conditions—in good lighting, close up, in a sober and attentive state of mind—such judgments are rarely, if ever, found to be mistaken. As Descartes put it, while our senses may deceive us in such cases, "there are many other facts as to which doubt is plainly impossible ... e.g. that I am here, sitting by the fire, wearing a winter cloak, holding this paper in my hands and so on..." (CSM II: 13).

Skeptical doubts are not, however, so easily dismissed. Descartes turns to the ideal case: he is clear-headed and attentive, seated by the fire, considering his body and cloak, his hands and the sheet of paper they hold. Any tendency to seriously question this, Descartes admits, might seem to be a sign of madness. But he recalls that there were many times when he thought he was truly perceiving his body and surroundings, only to wake up realizing that he was asleep in bed all along! If he felt so confident about such matters in his sleep, how could he trust his experiences now?

You believe that you are awake, reading this now. And you might respond that, unlike the sorts of experiences typical of dreams, your mind is clear, your present sensory experiences quite vivid, and the objects you perceive stable and familiar. Perhaps, as a matter of fact, dreams typically lack the clarity, vividness, and order of our waking life. (But ask yourself: how could you know this?) Even if this is actually true, it is not going to be enough to escape skepticism, for however much you are inclined to believe that you are awake, it is still possible that you are dreaming and so possible that your senses are highly misleading no matter how vivid they are. There is nothing incoherent in the supposition that you are having a very vivid and realistic dream; your having these very same experiences seems entirely consistent with the claim that you are merely dreaming. As Descartes says, no sensory experience can serve as a definitive sign or criterion that would allow you to tell whether or not you are dreaming. But how, on what basis, can you rule out that you are dreaming or that your senses are deceiving you? And if you cannot rule that out, how could you know anything about the external world—the world outside your mind—on the basis of your sensory or perceptual experiences?

While Descartes is not the first to present and discuss skeptical arguments in philosophy, he has certainly played a large role in making them central in epistemology.[2] Here's an attempt to make this skeptical argument explicit:

1   It is possible that I am dreaming.

2   If it is possible that I am dreaming, then I cannot know that I am not dreaming.

3   So, I cannot know that I am not dreaming.

4 If I cannot know that I am not dreaming, then I cannot know anything about the external world on the basis of perceptual experience.

5 So, I cannot know anything about the external world on the basis of perceptual experience.

The argument is deductively valid: (3) follows necessarily from (1) and (2), and (5) from (3) and (4). But are all the premises true? Premise (4) is highly plausible. What about (1) and (2)?

Premise (1) is difficult to resist, for while I may find that I can't help believing that I am awake, the supposition that I am merely dreaming seems logically consistent with my having just the sorts of experiences I do have. More carefully, that I am merely dreaming is consistent with my having experiences that are *intrinsically* just like the experiences I do have—indeed, it is consistent with my having any sort of experience or sequence of experiences, characterized in terms of their intrinsic features. My feelings of warmth and color, and my seeming to see a fire, are internal or intrinsic to my current experience itself; that the experience is produced by an actual fire, that it is simultaneous with a snowstorm, and other such relations or relational properties of the experience are not intrinsic to it, and not the sort of thing that I can determine directly just by examining my experience. It is important to see that the claim is not merely that dreams are possible, but that any experience I may have is consistent with and so leaves open the possibility that I am merely dreaming. As we have just seen, this is something Descartes accepts.

The hypothesis that I am merely dreaming is but one of indefinitely many skeptical hypotheses. Perhaps I am fed these experiences by an evil and very powerful demon, bent on deceiving me—another hypothetical scenario Descartes considers in the *First Meditation*. And there are more contemporary scenarios: Perhaps, rather than dreaming, I have ingested a powerful hallucinogen; I am not asleep, but my perceptual experiences still fail to match up with the external world. Or perhaps my body is floating in a pod (as in the movie *The Matrix*) or my brain floating in a vat, connected to some supercomputer controlled by a mad neuroscientist or advanced artificial intelligence. The underlying insight for (1) and its correlates for other scenarios is the same: it is possible that none of my sensory or perceptual experiences are trustworthy guides to the actual state of the world outside my mind.

What about premise (2)? Descartes seems to have thought that knowing that *P* requires being certain that *P*. Though this is a matter of some controversy, the certainty Descartes requires is arguably not merely psychological: it is not merely a matter of being fully confident or utterly without doubt as to the truth of *P*. Rather, for Descartes, knowing some proposition *P* requires *epistemic* certainty: having *evidence or reasons* that guarantee the truth of *P*. Given the possibility that I am dreaming, I cannot know that I am not dreaming.

To accept the conclusion (5) is to accept a kind of *skepticism*. We can distinguish varieties of skepticism in epistemology on the basis of (a) the particular kind of *epistemic status* (e.g., knowledge, justification, rationality, certainty, etc.) the skeptic is denying or challenging, and (b) the *scope* or *range* of skepticism, which determines the class of beliefs whose epistemic status is being denied or challenged. To accept (5) is to deny that I have, or even *can* have, any (a) knowledge of (b) the world outside my mind—at least the sort that is based on perceptual experience. It is doubtful though that I could acquire any knowledge of contingent facts about the external world without relying on perceptual experience. If this is right, then we can conclude from (5) that I cannot know any contingent facts about the external world.

Cartesian sources of foundational knowledge

Skepticism that targets knowledge of the external world is very broad in scope as compared to skepticism about, say, astrology, or evolution. But it is not *global skepticism*, for it does not deny that we have some knowledge. Descartes himself seems to have held that there are two ways of arriving at the truth that are not vulnerable to the dream argument, though he did not always distinguish explicitly between them. These are, moreover, sources of "foundational" knowledge, knowledge that does not depend on any inference or reasoning from other knowledge we already have.

First, there are truths that are known *a priori*—roughly, truths known not on the basis of sensory perception, but on the basis of pure reason or understanding. (These can also be contrasted with contingent truths known through *introspection*, a second source of foundational knowledge for Descartes. We will discuss this later in the present section.) We can know *a priori*, for example, that 2 + 3 = 5 and that triangles have three sides. Knowledge of these truths seems to depend purely on our grasp of the constituent ideas or concepts, and of the relations between them. Since such beliefs make no claim about what actually does exist in the external world, the trustworthiness (or lack thereof) of our perceptual experiences is not relevant to assessing them. As Descartes puts it, "for whether I am awake or asleep, two plus three make five, and a square does not have more than four sides" (CSM II: 29).

Interestingly, in the *First Meditation* Descartes entertains the possibility of going wrong even about such seemingly indubitable truths as these. Recall that he is attempting to subject as many of his beliefs to doubt in order to see what, if anything, remains standing, with the hope of building his knowledge on a more secure foundation. To that end, he considers the possibility that he is being deceived by someone extremely powerful, like God, or—since some may worry that such deception is incompatible with the nature of a perfect being—by an evil and very powerful demon. Is it not logically possible that there exists a powerful and evil demon bent on deceiving me not only in *my empirical* beliefs about the external world, based on some perceptual experience or observation, but also my *a priori* beliefs, even about apparently obvious "truths" of mathematics or geometry? We can construct an argument that is similar to the dream argument, the conclusion of which asserts *global* skepticism about knowledge:

1   It is possible that there exists a powerful and evil demon who is deceiving me not only in my empirical beliefs but also my *a priori* beliefs.

2   If it is possible that such an evil demon exists then I cannot know that I am not being deceived in my empirical and *a priori* beliefs.

3   So, I cannot know that I am not being deceived in my empirical and *a priori* beliefs.

4   If I cannot know that I am not being deceived in my empirical and *a priori* beliefs, then I cannot know anything.

5   So, I cannot know anything.

This too is a valid argument. Could the premises be challenged? In the *Second Meditation* Descartes comes to his famous insight: although the evil genius could deceive me about all sorts of things, he cannot deceive me into thinking that I don't exist. Why? For me to even wonder whether I am being deceived, I must exist. In order to doubt anything or think anything, I must exist. So "let him do his best at deception, he will never bring it about that I am nothing so long as I shall think that I am something" (CSM II: 30).

As some philosophers have noted, while thinking requires a thinker, it doesn't follow that the thinker is a *persisting* self.[3] Descartes cannot know, from the fact that some thought or experience now exists, that he exists as a persisting person; at best, he can conclude that a thinker, a subject of a thought, exists at that moment. Still, perhaps this rather modest foundation can do some work, or can be extended in some way.

Of course, it isn't just *thinking* or *experiencing* that requires existing: walking, sitting, eating, breathing, or just occupying space—these all require existing. But what, then, is so special about *thought*? Although Descartes is not explicit about this, the underlying point, presumably, is that when it comes to my own thoughts and experiences, I have a special sort of access to them. I can be *aware of them directly*, whereas I cannot be aware directly of walking, sitting, breathing, and so on. I can be aware that it *seems to me* that I am walking, sitting, or breathing, but not that I am *in fact* doing these things. So I know from my own case that there is thinking, and so, that there must be a present subject of this very thought.

How, then, shall we respond to the argument for global skepticism from the possibility of evil demon deception? We might claim that there is a kind of knowledge that is immune to doubt, knowledge made possible by a direct, transparent awareness of one's own thoughts, experiences, or conscious states. This knowledge is not empirical if by that we mean knowledge of the external world that is based on sense perception, and perhaps it does not always involve sensory or perceptual experience. But nor does it seem to be *a priori* knowledge, for it does not depend purely on an adequate grasp or understanding of the content of our thoughts, but on a grasp of the *existence* of our thoughts. It is a kind of *introspective* knowledge, arrived at by "looking in." This knowledge is still empirical in a broad sense: it is knowledge of contingent facts and depends on an awareness or consciousness of something's existence or presence. But, like *a priori* knowledge, this is knowledge that one can get "from the armchair," not knowledge that is based, directly or indirectly, on one's perceptions or observations of the external world. If we take "empirical knowledge" to include introspective knowledge, then this objection to the argument targets premise (1), for there is a kind of empirical judgment not undermined by the possibility of the evil demon. If, on the other hand, "empirical knowledge" is understood more narrowly as knowledge based at least in part on perceptual or sensory experience of the external world, then the objection targets premise (4), for even if the evil demon can deceive me with respect to my perceptual and *a priori* beliefs, that does not show that he can deceive me in all my introspective beliefs. In any case, this way of arriving at truths seems vulnerable to neither the dream argument nor the evil genius argument.

One might object that even if it is granted that one has knowledge of the existence of a thought, idea, experience, or conscious state, one cannot proceed from there to knowledge of the existence of a self—not even a possibly momentary or fleeting self. One must know that *thinking or thought requires a thinker*, which one can only know *a priori* if at all. If this is right, then it seems that knowledge of one's own existence depends on introspection (awareness of one's own ideas or experiences) *and* reason (*a priori* awareness that thinking requires a thinker). But the problem is that Descartes himself admits in the *First Meditation* that the evil demon could deceive one even about very simple *a priori* matters. Some question whether it is indeed true that we could be deceived about such simple *a priori* judgments as that $2 + 3 = 5$, that a triangle has three sides, or that thinking or thought requires a thinker. Indeed, Descartes' own considered view seems to be that when we focus on or attend to the simple abstract truths themselves, we can achieve a kind of insight into their truth that is so transparent that doubt about them is not possible (CSM II: 25, 48, 101). It is only when our attention is distracted by other things, including the very thought that an evil demon might be deceiving us, that we can be led to doubt such simple truths. In the *First Meditation* the meditator was easily distracted by such skeptical doubts. But after due reflection and adequate care, one can grasp ideas that are, as Descartes puts it, "clear and distinct," such that the possibility of error is ruled out and knowledge secured.

The study of the nature and scope of both our introspective knowledge and *a priori* knowledge are very important. But we focus in this chapter and in the rest of the book on the epistemology of *perception*, and on introspective and *a priori* knowledge only insofar as is relevant to these topics.

Descartes' response to skepticism regarding the external world

As we have seen, Descartes' search for secure foundations of knowledge led him to look inwardly, to his own ideas and experiences, for here things are as they seem and one can, at least sometimes, be certain of the existence of oneself and one's own ideas. Descartes, John Locke, George Berkeley, David Hume, and many other early modern philosophers accepted a thesis that is sometimes referred to as "the way of ideas": we lack direct awareness or direct perception of anything other than our own *ideas* (in a broad sense that includes thoughts and experiences of all sorts), and any perception or knowledge of other things depends in part on our awareness of our own ideas.

Descartes' explicit response to the dream argument comes at the very end of the *Meditations*. He attempts to bridge the epistemic gap between ideas and the external world by noticing the order and coherence among his experiences and apparent memories, and by appeal to knowledge of a non-deceiving God. For example, I seem to recall driving to Mt. Baker Park to do some reading while my kids play on the beach, and I also seem to recall driving a familiar route. I seem to perceive a park-like environment, just the sort that I am inclined to associate with "Mt. Baker Park." I am now apparently reading, watching my kids playing close by, and so on. It is possible that these experiences and apparent memories, while connected in such ways, are all misleading. But on Descartes' view we can know that God exists and that God is not a deceiver, and this gives us the assurance we need that this possibility is not actual, for God would not allow his careful and attentive subjects to be deceived.

Philosophers are generally, and understandably, unimpressed with Descartes' appeal to a non-deceiving God in this context. Any bit of doubt about God's existence, or God's not allowing me to be deceived in such a situation, would result in some doubt about whether I can trust my senses. Indeed, it seems implausible that we could ever be *epistemically certain* of any of our beliefs regarding the external world.

Hume and the deepening of skepticism

Perhaps we can block the argument by denying that knowledge requires epistemic certainty. Many have complained that Descartes' requirement of certainty is too demanding. Why can't beliefs that are based on very good but not fully conclusive reasons count as knowledge? Moreover, suppose we have no knowledge of the external world—either because Descartes is right that knowledge requires certainty or because, perhaps, we fail some other condition of knowledge. Still, are we not in some way *rational* or *justified* in our beliefs regarding the external world? Perhaps we have, all things considered, inconclusive but still very good reasons to believe, and whether or not these beliefs constitute knowledge is a further question.

We shall return to the question of whether knowledge requires certainty briefly later in the book (Chapter 4). But, as David Hume (1711–76) realized, the threat of skepticism runs deeper, challenging not just Cartesian certainty but even rational or justified belief in the external world, and any view of knowledge of the external world that requires justified belief.

Since I recognize that skeptical hypotheses are consistent with my having the experiences that I do, I cannot just assume that I can rely on my experiences to get the world right: *I need some reason to think that my perceptual or sensory experiences are trustworthy or reliable guides to the state of the external world.* But I cannot rely on my perceptual experiences themselves in order to acquire such a reason. To rely on perceptual experiences in order to determine whether my perceptual experiences are trustworthy is viciously circular; I can only rely on them if I *already* know, or at least have good reason to believe, that they are trustworthy. Moreover, I cannot rely on understanding or reason alone to determine whether my perceptual experiences are trustworthy, for, as Hume emphasized, pure reason or understanding is concerned with what is possible and what is necessary, and not with contingent matters such as the reliability or trustworthiness of our perceptual experiences. And there seems no other way available to determine the trustworthiness of my experiences. I cannot peer behind my ideas as though they were a veil between myself and the world, and check if they correspond to the way things are. So, if it is indeed possible that my perceptual experiences are not trustworthy guides to the state of the world outside my mind, whether because I am dreaming, hallucinating, am the victim of a deceiver, or whatever, then I cannot know that they are trustworthy. Indeed, the upshot of the argument seems to be that I cannot have any more reason to believe that my senses are trustworthy (that I am awake, not being deceived, etc.) than that they are not!

We can summarize the argument in the following way:

1   My external world beliefs are rational or justified only if I have good reasons to take my perceptual experiences to be trustworthy or reliable guides to the state of the world outside my mind.

2   I cannot acquire such a reason by examining the external world directly in order to determine whether my ideas correspond to it, for I have no such direct access; any access I have is by way of my ideas or experiences.

3   I cannot acquire such reasons by relying on the very perceptual experiences whose trustworthiness is being questioned, for that would be viciously circular.

4   I cannot acquire such reasons purely *a priori*, for reason or understanding alone cannot inform me about the reliability or trustworthiness of my perceptual experiences.

5   There is no other way to acquire such a reason.

6   Therefore, my external world beliefs are not justified.

The skeptical problem thus seems to challenge not only the sort of knowledge of the external, physical world that Descartes is after in the *Meditations*, which requires *certainty*, but even the position that our belief in the external world is rational or justified. In effect, Descartes' reply to this skeptical argument targets premise (4), for he holds that we can determine *a priori* that God exists and that God would not allow us to be deceived when we attend carefully to our ideas and the relations between them. But for those who doubt that we have good reasons *a priori* to believe that a God exists who would not allow us to be deceived in these matters—let alone reasons that yield epistemic certainty—this response to skepticism won't help us avoid the conclusion that we lack rational or justified belief in the external world.

1 Descartes seems to think, in the context of the *Meditations*, that knowledge requires certainty. Is this right? Can you think of reasons to accept that knowledge does require certainty? Can you think of reasons to deny it?

2 Descartes apparently takes at least some of our introspective judgments, judgments about some of our own ideas or experiences, to be certain or infallible. Are there some sorts of judgments about your experiences that are fallible? Can you imagine a case in which you believe something about your experiences that is false? Is there something about these cases that explains why they are false—perhaps some sort of confusion, or something corresponding to a lack of "clarity and distinctness"?

3 Consider the Humean skeptical argument offered toward the end of the chapter. Is there any premise of the argument that you are inclined to deny? Can you think of an objection to that premise?

Descartes' *Meditations on First Philosophy* (1641) is essential reading, especially the *First, Second*, and *Sixth Meditations*. For Hume's skeptical doubts and arguments, see his *Enquiry Concerning Human Understanding* (1748) sections 1–5, especially section 4. Russell's *Problems of Philosophy* (1912: Ch. 1 and 2) provides a classical and accessible discussion of skepticism, and a critical evaluation of some of Descartes's arguments. Newman's entry on "Descartes' Epistemology" in the *Stanford Encyclopedia of Philosophy* (2014) provides a detailed discussion and many resources.

2

Realism, idealism, and common sense

This chapter continues to set the stage with the historical background to contemporary debates, beginning with an examination of Locke's responses to the skeptic. His causal explanation reply, essentially an early version of the abductivist reply we discuss later in the book, is discussed in some detail, found potentially promising, but in need of development and still vulnerable to skeptical concerns. We also examine a few key disagreements between Locke and Berkeley related to metaphysical and epistemological problems of perception, including Locke's primary/secondary quality distinction and the related argument from perceptual relativity, and Berkeley's attempt to defend idealism. We end by considering Reid's concern with the privileging of introspection and reason over other sources of knowledge by the early modern philosophers, and his own response to skepticism. We also see that Reid's epistemology of perception seems to be an early version of epistemological externalism.

In the previous chapter we introduced the problem of skepticism about the external world through an examination of Descartes' *Meditations on First Philosophy*. We briefly discussed the shortcomings of Descartes' reply to skepticism, and how the skeptical concerns regarding Cartesian knowledge seem to extend quite easily to rational or justified belief. In this chapter we look at some historically influential attempts to respond to skepticism and vindicate common sense by Locke, Berkeley, and Reid. As we shall see, however, Hume's skeptical concerns remain a formidable obstacle to these attempts to vindicate common sense.

Locke's replies to the skeptic

John Locke (1632–1704) held that the highest "degree of certainty" attaches to "intuitive knowledge" and to the conclusions of deductively valid inferences from our intuitive knowledge, "demonstrative knowledge." Locke's notion of "intuitive knowledge" seems to include *a priori* knowledge of self-evident truths, e.g., simple mathematical and geometric truths. But at least sometimes he uses the label broadly to include introspective knowledge or what Locke calls knowledge "by reflection": we can attend to or notice directly our own present experiences and ideas. Locke seems to agree with Descartes that we can be absolutely certain of some contingent truths about our own existence, and the existence of our own ideas or experiences. Like the early modern philosophers generally, he accepted the "way of ideas": we are directly aware of our own ideas (including sensations, thoughts, and mental states of various sorts), and can have knowledge of the external world only by being aware of our own ideas. He admits that beliefs about particular objects and events in the external world based on the senses lack the degree of certainty attainable by intuition and demonstration, and so fall short of Descartes' standard for knowledge. However, he claims that the degree of certainty we have when it comes to these beliefs is not "mere probability," but yields as much certainty or assurance as we need for practical purposes, and so also deserves to be called "knowledge" (Bk.IV.Ch.ii).[1]

It is a matter of some controversy how we should understand Locke's response to skepticism. Rather than attempt to settle on a particular interpretation, we will examine a few strands or themes in Locke's work that have been highly influential.

The mocking reply

Locke seems much less worried and open to skepticism regarding the senses than Descartes is in the *Meditations*. He doubts that anyone could really be "so skeptical as to be uncertain of the existence of those things which he sees and feels" and ridicules the skeptic as one who "will never have any controversy with me, since he can never be sure I say anything contrary to his own opinion" (Bk.IV.Ch.xi.3). If there is an objection here, it seems to be that the skeptic's position is in some sense self-defeating, and so the skeptic's own reasoning and arguments are without force: "where all is but a dream, reasoning and arguments are of no use, truth and knowledge nothing" (Bk. IV.Ch.ii.14). Locke thus seems to regard skepticism about the external world to be self-defeating, not in the sense of being incoherent or contradictory, but in the sense that if skepticism is true then one cannot know or even be justified in believing it.

These attempts to mock the skeptic and show that the skeptic's position is self-defeating don't make for very satisfactory responses to skepticism. First, it's not clear that the skeptic's position here really is self-defeating. The position of *global* skepticism about knowledge—the view that we do not have any knowledge—is self-defeating because it asserts that it is impossible to know *anything*, and so impossible to know even that global skepticism is true. By denying that we can know anything at all, by inference or otherwise, all arguments or forms of persuasion are, by the skeptic's own lights, useless as a means to knowledge. But while global skepticism is self-defeating in this way, external world skepticism is not in any obvious way self-defeating. The skeptic who challenges Locke's claim to knowledge of the external world might grant that he cannot help but believe in what he seems to see or feel, and so cannot help but believe that he is conversing with Locke, but may yet doubt whether these beliefs do indeed constitute knowledge, and present skeptical arguments like the dream argument to support this claim. So long as nothing asserted in the dream argument requires knowledge of the external world, it's not clear that the charge of self-defeat applies. The same might be said of external world skepticism about rational or justified belief.[2]

Second: The fact that *the skeptic* may be unsure that Locke and others exist or ever say anything contrary to his own opinion seems irrelevant. Even *if* the skeptic's own position is self-defeating, that alone provides no good reason to think that skepticism is false. Insofar as we consider and accept the possibility, in principle, that we are dreaming or that our senses deceive us in some way, the question of whether we have good reason to hold that we are not deceived naturally arises. Whether or not we can convince or persuade *someone else* who is skeptical is irrelevant. It may help to recall the distinction between a *merely psychological* degree of certainty or confidence, and an *epistemic* one; granted that we can't help being psychologically confident in our beliefs, the interesting question is whether this confidence is *rational or justified*, at least to some extent—whether we have and can articulate good reasons for taking our external world beliefs to be true.

The common sense reply

So, why should we trust our own sensory experiences when we recognize the possibility that they are terribly misleading? One response Locke seems to give, and perhaps it is the underlying motivation behind the mocking reply above as well, is to say that it's just *obvious* or *common sense* that we do indeed know by way of our sensory or perceptual experiences of them that particular objects exist. Sure, we cannot have the same degree of certainty that our senses do not deceive us, or that they correspond to the way things are, as we do of our own existence, but our senses themselves just obviously do give us enough evidence to count as knowledge. We have "assurance... from our senses themselves, that they do not err in the information they give us of the existence of things without us ..." (Bk.IV.Ch.xi.3).

Without further development, however, this response is unsatisfactory. First, it just invites the question: why should we trust what we regard as obvious or common sense? It may be that we can't help but rely on our sensory faculties, that they are the best, the only, sort of evidence we can have for the existence of other things, but that does not show that they provide *good* evidence for the existence of other things. Second and relatedly, even if it is sometimes appropriate to hold that a belief obviously counts as knowledge, or is justified, the philosopher is interested in understanding *why* the belief has this epistemic status. If it is possible for the senses to deceive, what is it about these senses that provide this epistemic status? We don't yet have a clear answer to that question.[3]

The causal explanation reply

Although Locke apparently accepts something like the view that the senses themselves are, on their own, good enough to provide what is needed, he also offers "concurrent" or additional reasons to "further confirm" our assurance (Bk.IV.Ch.xi.3). Rather than merely take the senses at face value, the strategy here is to point to particular features and regularities experienced that call out for explanation, and to infer, from the fact that we have such experiences, that particular external things exist and are their causes. In contemporary terms, these arguments seem to take the form of an *inference to the best explanation*: we have such-and-such experiences; the best explanation of our having these experiences is that they are caused by external objects of such-and-such a sort; therefore, external objects of this sort exist. These arguments are not intended to yield what Locke calls "demonstrative knowledge"; that is, they do not provide the degree of assurance or certainty of conclusions arrived at by deductively valid inferences from intuitive or self-evident truths. Still, they might provide enough assurance in the conclusion to yield knowledge or at least rational belief.

The use of an explanatory argument suggests an objection to the Humean skeptical argument from the previous chapter. We have no way to verify directly, by an awareness of the external world itself, that our perceptual experiences correspond to the way the world is. But perhaps we can make an explanatory inference from our having certain experiences or "ideas" to the existence of external objects as their causes. The Humean argument seemed to just rule this out in claiming that there is no other way to justify the reliability or trustworthiness of our sensory experiences. (As we shall see, Hume wouldn't be satisfied with this response.)

But are such arguments available? Locke offers four arguments of this form. The first is *the argument from the need for organs of sense.* Those that lack functioning sensory organs cannot have the ideas belonging to that sense produced in their minds; "this is too evident to be doubted" (Bk.IV.Ch.xi.4). But those that have functioning sense organs do not automatically have ideas belonging to that sense; they only have them in certain circumstances. People do not experience vivid colors in the dark, or taste fruit without eating some, and so on for other senses. These ideas of ours are best explained as resulting from the operation of external objects on our sensory organs.

The second is *the argument from unavoidable or involuntary ideas.* There are some ideas that are voluntary, under my control, or avoidable, and others that are not, even when the ideas are about the same things. To use one of Locke's examples, I can think of the sun, and of light, with my eyes closed. And I can, with ease, direct my mind to ideas of other things. But sometimes I have other ideas—vivid sensations—of the sun and light. These ideas seem to force themselves upon me, and I cannot avoid having them. Therefore, these ideas are not the mere product of my own memory or imagination, or other actions of my own mind, but must have an external cause.

The third is *the argument from pleasure and pain.* Pain and discomfort accompany my ideas of hot and cold, thirst and hunger, etc., sometimes, not always. What explains this difference, and the similar difference that pleasure sometimes does and other times does not accompany certain ideas? The explanation appears to be that in some cases the ideas are the product of memory, thought, or imagination, while at other times the ideas and the accompanying pains or pleasures are due to the action of external objects on our bodies.

Unfortunately, these arguments are either question-begging or fail to secure a non-skeptical conclusion. The argument from the need for sensory organs is most clearly question-begging. How could we know that those who lack functioning organs do not have the corresponding sensations or ideas, or that those that do have functioning sense organs only have these sensations when the relevant objects are present? It does not seem that we could know such things *a priori*, but to rely on our observations of other people or their testimony is to assume that our senses are trustworthy or reliable. Moreover, hallucinations and dreams seem to involve experiences that are not caused (at least directly) by the employment of sense organs, so there is a prima facie case that sense organs are not essential to various sorts of experiences. The second and third arguments, while not obviously question-begging, don't clearly yield the conclusion that the cause must be *external to the mind*. Why, after all, can't the cause of our unavoidable ideas be purely internal, in the way that some unavoidable ideas that we have during sleep or when delirious with a fever seem to us to be unavoidable? Similarly, perhaps the cause of pain or pleasure experienced is internal—indeed, perhaps the relative vividness of sensations of hot and cold account for the pain or discomfort we feel, and the abstractness or lack of vividness of our thoughts of hot and cold account for the lack of pain; or perhaps there is some other internal cause, besides imagination or memory, that is responsible for this.

But even if we set aside these worries, there is a further problem that afflicts all the first three arguments: even granting that *some external cause* is required to explain these features of our experiences, there is no reason offered to think that the external cause must correspond, even roughly, to our ideas of them. The skeptic can grant for sake of argument that these features of experience require external causes, but ask why we should think that the cause is even approximately as we take it to be.

The fourth is *the argument from coherence and prediction*. This is the most interesting of Locke's four reasons, though it also seems to incorporate some of the experiential features appealed to above (like unavoidability). "Our senses," Locke says, "in many cases bear witness to the truth of each other's report, concerning the existence of sensible things without us" (Bk. IV.Ch.xi.7). Of course, talk of the senses "bearing witness" to each other's "reports" cannot be taken literally; persons, not experiences, can make reports and witness the reports of others. Still, the underlying idea seems to be, roughly, that when we consider the many distinct sensory experiences that we have over time, we see that, together, they provide a largely coherent picture or representation of a physical world. The fact that these experiences "fit together" in this inevitably incomplete but largely coherent way calls out for explanation. The best explanation seems to be that there is a world external to my mind that is, in at least some central respects, as it seems to be.

For example, I now seem to see a roughly cylindrical object (a coffee mug) filled with some liquid, located slightly ahead of me and to the left. My visual experience of this object over time is relatively stable—I seem to be presented, from different perspectives as I seem to move about in this room, with the same cylindrical object. And when I attempt to reach for it, I seem to see a hand move towards it and apparently touch it, and I have a tactile sensation of a cylindrical object, one that matches the visual sensation. I can also intend to tap on the object, and to move it with my hand and bring it up to my mouth, and I find that I have the very sensations of sight, sound, touch, and taste that I should expect to have if the object and my body do indeed exist. I can apparently repeat these actions, and when I do I have similar patterns of experience, whether I want to have them or not. (See Locke's *Essay*, Bk.IV.Ch.xi.7, for some of his own examples.) The best explanation of this "coherence" of sorts between various sensory ideas or appearances seems to be that there exist particular objects having at least roughly the properties they perceptually seem to us to have.

Primary and secondary qualities, and the argument from perceptual relativity

We have to be careful, though, about which sensed properties to apply to external world objects. Like Descartes and many other early modern philosophers, Locke affirms that objects have certain "primary qualities" like shape, size, location, solidity, and quantity or number. We have ideas corresponding to these qualities. These ideas of primary qualities of bodies are, Locke says, "resemblances of them, and their patterns really do exist in the bodies themselves ..." (Bk.II.Ch.viii.15). The argument from coherence and prediction in the previous section might be used to support this: our visual and tactile appearances of primary qualities of objects like their shape and size seem relatively stable and coherent.

We also have ideas (sensory experiences) of qualities like *color, sound, smell, taste, and (degree of) heat*. But Locke follows Descartes in denying that physical objects have qualities that resemble these ideas. The basic argument for this, sometimes called the *argument from perceptual relativity*, is that such sensed qualities change with change in the perceiver's conditions, so that they cannot all resemble or correspond to the same objects. And there seems to be no principled or non-arbitrary way to determine which of the ideas resemble or correspond to the actual qualities of objects. It follows that the objects themselves either fail to resemble our ideas—this seems to be Locke's conclusion—or, more modestly, that even if some of these do apply, there is no way for us to tell which specific qualities the objects really do have.

Consider, for example, the fact that the same foods can taste different at different times, depending on such factors as what you ate right before, the condition of your palate, or your state of health. And it is quite plausible that to different species, and perhaps even to different individuals of the same species, some of the same foods taste very different. If the tastes we experience at different times are qualities of the object itself, then the object itself must be changing in these varying conditions. That would be a rather odd kind of change. Moreover, it would still lead us to attribute conflicting qualities to the same food when it tastes differently to different individuals. It seems much more plausible to assume that "taste" is really a quality of our own minds or experiences and not a quality of the objects themselves.

Or consider the fact that the color of an object seems to change with change in lighting conditions and viewing angle. It is logically possible that these colors of objects actually change depending on the conditions, and perhaps even depending on who is observing it. But if color is a quality of the object itself, that would be an odd kind of change. Moreover, it would still lead us to attribute conflicting colors to objects when viewed by different individuals, from different angles. It would be odd to claim that only certain organisms or individuals have experiences that capture the true color of the surrounding objects. There doesn't seem to be a principled or non-arbitrary way to determine what angle, under which conditions, etc., will reveal the true color of the object. It follows that the objects themselves either fail to resemble the colors we experience—this seems to be Locke's conclusion—or else there is simply no way to tell which colors the objects really do have.

There is a sense in which an object, like an apple, does genuinely have the "secondary quality" of color. Locke takes a secondary quality of an object to be a power or disposition that the object has to produce certain ideas in us, but where the idea produced does not resemble anything in the object itself. An apple might have the power to produce an idea or sensation of red in subjects like me, and in this sense we can speak loosely of its being "red" even when no one is looking at it—for even then, it has the *power* to produce a sensation of red. Locke also seems to think that we have good reason to suspect that it is in part in virtue of certain insensible or microscopic physical properties of the object or its surface that it has this power to produce such ideas in me. But my sensation of red does not resemble any of these properties. Similarly with other secondary qualities: Locke can say that a pineapple is "sweet", but only in the sense that it has the power or disposition to produce an idea or sensation of that familiar quality of sweetness in certain conditions, in organisms like ourselves.

Berkeley's critique of Locke

George Berkeley (1685–1753) forcefully criticized Locke's views of the nature of physical objects and his anti-skeptical arguments (*Principles* I.8–20).[4] He grants for sake of argument that it is *possible* for material or physical objects corresponding to our ideas to exist and cause these ideas in us, but asks how we may *know* this.[5] Berkeley explicitly considers the attempt to "explain" how ideas are produced "by supposing external bodies in their likeness rather than otherwise," so that "it might be at least probable there are such things ..." (*Principles* I.20). He points out that proponents of such arguments themselves admit that they do not know how, in principle, material things can produce an idea in the mind, let alone how the specific sorts of ideas we have are produced. How, then, can they have any confidence that the external causes correspond to our ideas of them? Indeed, Berkeley complains, isn't it at least as plausible that a supreme being, like God, is responsible for these ideas and has chosen to create them in us without a complex world of material things as their intermediaries?

One might reply on Locke's behalf that knowledge of exactly how these ideas are produced is not required. Perhaps we can have good reasons to think that some of our ideas are produced by the corresponding objects without knowing exactly how this takes place. The fact that our ideas of objects, at least of their primary qualities, are stable across a range of conditions provides us with such reasons.

But Berkeley claims, against Locke, that the argument from perceptual relativity applies just as much to primary qualities. Our ideas or experiences of primary qualities such as size and shape also change with change in conditions of perception. What you believe to be a table top, for example, will present you with very different shapes and sizes from different perspectives, and there seems to be no way to decide which of these many varying shapes and sizes applies to the object, if any. We may be inclined to treat these different ideas as ideas of one and the same object, and call it a "rectangular" top, but it only appears rectangular from very few perspectives. Why should we trust this inclination? Given the changes in size and shape with apparent change in perspective, why should I trust that there is an object over there that has a rectangular top?

It is difficult to find a clear answer from Locke. But there is a tempting and natural answer, one that is at least suggested by some of what Locke says (e.g., see Bk.II.Ch.ix). What we experience certainly varies from different perspectives, but in just the ways we should expect if the table has a rectangular top. It is a matter of perspective and geometry: a rectangular top will look rectangular if viewed from directly above; it will look like a trapezoid or other non-rectangular quadrilateral from various other perspectives; and it will look smaller the farther away one is from the object. Various other such cues can help us narrow down at least some of the primary qualities that the object has.[6]

Even if this is successful as a response to the problem of perceptual or perspectival relativity, Berkeley might still ask what reason we have to believe that there exist mind-independent objects with these primary qualities rather than holding that the ideas that exhibit this coherence are caused in us by God. The possibility that there is a God—or an evil genius—producing these ideas in us remains, and it seems we need a clearer reason to think the Lockean hypothesis is more probable than the God hypothesis or evil genius hypothesis.

Berkeley's idealism

The previous section might give one the impression that Berkeley is on the side of the skeptic. This is not right. On Berkeley's view, we do know that such things as books, mountains, and trees exist. But Berkeley is an *idealist* about the nature of these objects: they are essentially *mental* or *mind-dependent*; for such objects, "to be is to be perceived." Berkeley seems to think of ordinary physical objects as *ideas*, or rather, *bundles or collections of ideas*: "Thus, for example, a certain colour, taste, smell, figure and consistence having been observed to go together, are accounted one distinct thing, signified by the name apple. Other collections of ideas constitute a stone, a tree, a book, and the like sensible things ..." (*Principles* I.1).

Berkeley motivates his idealism in part by arguing that the alternative, Cartesian and Lockean view of ordinary objects as mind-independent entities leads inevitably to skepticism. If one wants to avoid skepticism and preserve the commonsense view that we can know about such objects by perceiving them, then perhaps it is best to be an idealist: if there is no ontological gap between our ideas and ordinary objects, then perhaps there is no epistemological gap either.

Despite Berkeley's attempt to preserve common sense, the view seems to conflict with core parts of what the ordinary subject believes. One problem is that it seems we have to give up the view that different subjects can observe or perceive the very same object. We each perceive our own ideas only, not the ideas others have in their heads, even if there is a similarity between these ideas. Berkeley responds at one point that while in a "philosophical" sense the objects perceived are not strictly identical, not one and the same thing, there is another, more common, "vulgar" sense in which the objects perceived count as the same: they are very similar.[7] But, against Berkeley, it could be argued that people are well aware of the distinction between the two senses of "same." When I tell you that my partner and I have the same car, you might naturally wonder whether I mean that we own only one car or have two cars of the same kind.

Berkeley's idealism also seems to conflict with the commonsense view that these ordinary objects persist, even when we cease to have the ideas associated with them. For example, I just turned away from my computer for a moment to look out the window to my left, and I believe, commonsensically, that the computer remains there. But if I am not having the relevant ideas (I do not observe the figures and colors I associate with my "computer") and no other perceiver is in the room, then those ideas do not exist, and so the computer they constitute does not exist either. One reaction to this problem is to offer an analysis of objects involving subjunctive conditionals with possibly false or "counterfactual" (contrary to fact) antecedents. Berkeley himself seems at times to offer such an analysis: "The table I write on, I say, exists; that is, I see and feel it; and if I were out of my study, I should say it existed—meaning by that that if I was in my study I might perceive it, or that some other spirit actually does perceive it" (*Principles* I.3). Roughly, to say that there is a table in front of one is just to say that your actual or possible experiences are constrained in certain ways. Thus, according to this view, for there to exist a table even when you are not perceiving one is for it to be true that you might or would perceive it under certain circumstances. This does not quite fit Berkeley's slogan that "to be is to be perceived" (*esse est percipi*). Perhaps the slogan is not to be read literally; perhaps "to be is to be the *actual or possible* object of perception" is closer. However, as this amended slogan highlights, Berkeley's account raises questions about what it is for something to be a merely possible object, and whether accepting such entities is compatible with his idealism.

Perhaps there is a different strategy available to Berkeley. To say that the table exists is to say *that some spirit actually perceives it*. When no finite beings like ourselves are appropriately related to the table to perceive it, it must be that there is some much more powerful being—on Berkeley's view, God—holding these ideas in mind. And if it is pointed out that God cannot literally have the very ideas we have in our minds, perhaps there is never-theless a looser sense in which our ideas and some of God's ideas are "the same" (i.e., similar).

Berkeley attempts to motivate idealism in part by claiming that it can, and the materialist views cannot, avoid skepticism about commonsense knowledge—if there is no ontological gap between our ideas and ordinary objects, then perhaps there is no epistemological gap either. But we can now appreciate that matters are more complex, for these ordinary objects are not simple ideas we can be directly aware of at once, but bundles or collections of ideas that have to be related in certain ways, and have a degree of stability and persistence that is not directly observable. Still, Berkeley seems to think that even if we grant for sake of argument that material or mind-independent objects are possible, and rely on a kind of *inference to the best explanation* to account for the nature of our own ideas or experiences, the idealist does better: the forceful and patterned nature of many of my ideas can be accounted for by the existence of persisting objects (bundles of ideas) in some other mind with the capacity to hold fixed a more complete and elaborate collection of ideas than our finite minds are capable of. There is thus a sense in which even for Berkeley some ideas are merely products of our own minds (e.g., the fleeting ideas we associate with dreams), while others have a more stable source outside of us—in the mind of God.

Besides arguing that the alternative view of objects as mind-independent leads inevitably to skepticism, Berkeley argues for idealism in more direct ways. The most direct is his famous "master argument" (*Principles* I.22–3). The argument is deceptively simple. The Lockean claims that it is possible for an object to exist without being perceived, conceived, or thought of by anyone. But to take this to be possible is to conceive of something that is unconceived, which is a contradiction: you cannot conceive of something that is not conceived by anyone—*you* are conceiving it even if no one else is. Having arrived at a contradiction, we should reject the assumption that led to it: no, it is not possible for something to exist unconceived.

The argument has a serious flaw, however. It is of course true that I cannot conceive of some possible object, like a tree, without having an idea that is about it or that represents it. In that sense, I cannot conceive of something that is, in fact, not conceived by me. But that is trivial. How is that supposed to show that it is incoherent to think of the *possibility* that a tree exists without someone's having an idea about it? In thinking about this possibility, I am having an idea of a tree, but *my having an idea* of a tree is not part of what I am thinking *about*—in fact, I am thinking about the possibility that there is a tree that is *not* conceived of by anyone, that there is *no idea anyone has* of it. That is the sort of possibility that my idea is about, and that idea has not been shown to be incoherent or contradictory. The argument will be tempting only if one does not distinguish carefully between *the mental representation* and *what it represents or is about*, between that which we conceive *with* and that which we conceive *of*.

But perhaps the underlying argument is really just an appeal to phenomenology, an appeal to what it is like to have thoughts or ideas of such things.[8] Although the explicit argument Berkeley gives is not successful, perhaps the underlying point, badly stated there, is that when we try to conceive of something existing without there being a perceiver or mind that conceives it, we find ourselves unable to do so. For example, when we imagine or think of a tree, it is always *from some apparent perspective or other*, or *as experienced or perceived in this way or that*, and we find we cannot keep this subjective or perspectival aspect from being part of what is conceived or imagined. If so, the underlying worry is connected with Berkeley's skepticism about the mind's ability to attend to properties or qualities of objects and consider them *abstractly*, independently of any mental or psychological features. He claims, for example, that we cannot conceive of objects having primary qualities like shape and size independently of qualities like color, that we cannot imagine a tree without imagining that it also has some color or other (*Principles* I.10). And if the Lockean accepts that these qualities are mind-dependent, and that they are, as Berkeley puts it, "inseparable" from primary qualities, then the primary qualities must be mind-dependent as well.

Not everyone will agree with Berkeley about the limits of abstraction. They may also raise serious worries about how he could make sense of our ability to think in general terms—for example, about all triangles, as when we attempt to prove some of their properties in geometry. Berkeley claims that an idea, which in itself is particular, becomes general by being made to represent or stand for all other particular ideas of the same sort. (*Principles*, Intro.12). But how one idea—say, a particular triangular image or the word "triangle"—could be made to represent or stand for all particular triangles is precisely the crucial question, a question that Berkeley never answers.

Reid's response to skepticism

As we have seen above, avoiding skepticism about knowledge, and even rational or justified belief, was a significant challenge for the early modern philosophers. Insofar as Descartes, Locke, and even Berkeley rely on some sort of inference or reasoning from our own ideas or experiences to the existence of ordinary objects, the skeptic is likely to raise questions about our justification for this inference. What reason do we have for thinking that this inference is legitimate?

Hume would probably motivate the skeptical worry by presenting the following dilemma: the inference from what I know about my own sensory experiences or "impressions" to their unobserved causes must either be *a priori* or *a posteriori*. The inference cannot be *a priori*, for purely *a priori* inferences are *demonstrative or deductive*—they *entail* their conclusions—and the inference from my experiences to the existence of objects is not deductive, since it is logically possible that I have these experiences in the absence of these objects. But nor can the legitimacy of the inference be justified *a posteriori or empirically*, for then we would be relying either on past perceptions, other explanatory inferences, or both, and so assuming that our perceptions are trustworthy, that our explanatory inferences are warranted, or both.

Hume's skepticism thus runs deep. Indeed, Hume's contemporary, Thomas Reid (1710–96), took Hume to have successfully shown that skepticism regarding the external world is inevitable if we accept only introspection and reason as our legitimate sources of knowledge. In fact, Reid took the skeptical consequences to be even more serious, for if we can only be directly aware of our present ideas, and we must use reason to infer everything else we know, then it is difficult to see how we could justify belief in past events, other minds, or even the existence of a self. The worry is that reason on its own is unable to bridge that gap with so meager a ground or foundation.

Reid saw that the debate over skepticism depended heavily on the privileging of these two sources—introspection or what he called "consciousness", and reason—over other sources like perception and memory. While the skeptic demands to be given a reason why perception should be trusted, where it is assumed that introspection and reason are trustworthy, Reid counters with the question of why reason, or even consciousness or introspection, should be trusted over perception. And he seems to have held that no good reason can be given to trust any one of these fundamental belief-forming sources or dispositions over others:

> Why, sir, should I believe the faculty of reason more than that of perception? They both came out of the same shop, and were made by the same artist; and if he put one piece of false ware into my hands, what should hinder him from putting another? [1764/1997: Ch. 6, Sec. 2.]

> Thus the faculties of consciousness, of memory, of external sense, and of reason, are equally the gifts of nature. No good reason can be assigned for receiving the testimony of one of them, which is not of equal force with regard to the others. The greatest sceptics admit the testimony of consciousness, and allow what it testifies to be held as a first principle. If, therefore, they reject the immediate testimony of sense or of memory, they are guilty of an inconsistency. [1785/2002: Essay VI, Ch. 4]

Why can no good reason be given to trust one of these sources as opposed to any other? Reid sometimes seems to hold that the skeptics accept these sources because they find certain beliefs irresistible—they find themselves convinced, and cannot help but believe, certain fundamental principles of logic for example. But then, if we find ourselves convinced, or find it psychologically irresistible to believe that certain objects exist, on what grounds can the skeptics claim that their convictions are trustworthy but the conviction that these objects exist is not? If our convictions in principles of logic are a sign that we are latching on to some truth, why shouldn't it be a sign in the case of perception as well?

The claim that the skeptics and early modern philosophers are ultimately relying only on a psychological conviction or confidence is controversial. (Indeed, as we shall see in a moment, Reid himself seems to think there is more to our trust in reason and introspection than this.) So it would help to motivate the concern of arbitrariness in some other way. Though Reid does not put the worry in this way, the basic argument can be put in the form of a dilemma. If there is a good reason to trust *a priori* reason or introspection over other sources, that reason will have to either come from *a priori* reason or introspection (or their combination) on the one hand, or have some other source on the other. If the reason's source is the former, then we are just assuming that they are legitimate and superior sources, and so begging the question. If the reason comes from some other source, then we are relying on that other source in order to support the claim that it is inferior to reason and introspection, which is incoherent. The privileging of *a priori* reason and introspection on the part of the early modern philosophers, skeptics and non-skeptics alike, is therefore unmotivated or arbitrary. They must either reject all these fundamental sources and be stuck with global skepticism, or treat sources like perception and memory on a par with reason and introspection.

Reid himself is no skeptic. He takes all these fundamental sources, including perception, to be legitimate "first principles." Beliefs about the external world are justified by our acts of perceiving, beliefs about the past are justified by our acts of remembering, and so on, without the need for any *reasoning or inference* from the nature of our ideas, impressions, or representations to these beliefs.[9] He thus seems to accept quite explicitly what Locke *perhaps* accepted implicitly: that some beliefs about the external world are foundationally justified. They depend for their justification on acts of perception, but there is no need for us to form beliefs about the nature of our own experiences and reason our way to conclusions about the reliability of our perceptions or the presence of objects in the external world.

Of course, not everyone will agree with Reid that there is no good reason to privilege reason and introspection over perception. As we have seen, Descartes didn't simply assume that reason and introspection were trust-worthy. In fact, in a number of places, Reid himself grants that introspection and reason are epistemically superior in a way that is difficult to square with his criticism of the early modern philosophers. He claims that some necessary truths are grasped in such a way that the "light of truth so fills my mind, in these cases, that I can neither conceive nor desire anything more satisfying" (1785/2002: Essay II, Ch. 4). He also says that our consciousness of our own sensations is such that it is impossible that these sensations should not be real (1785/2002: Essay II, Ch. 22), and even says that "from this source of consciousness is derived all that we know," that "there is no branch of knowledge that stands upon a firmer foundation; for surely no kind of evidence can go beyond that of consciousness" (1785/2002: Essay VI, Ch. 5). Reid thus seems to grant that reason and introspection can provide the most satisfying, most complete assurance of the truth possible. Perhaps this is compatible with regarding perception as a legitimate, independent source of belief, provided that one allows, as Reid does, that foundational beliefs be fallible. Still, these admissions seem to weaken his case against the privileging of introspection and reason over perception.[10]

What alternative, positive account of the epistemology of perception is Reid offering? It is instructive to compare Reid with Locke. As we have seen,

Locke seems to take our knowledge of physical objects to depend on our awareness of our own ideas or sensations, and on the *resemblance* between these ideas and some of the qualities of physical objects. Reid denies that there is any such resemblance; he follows Berkeley in claiming that "nothing is like an idea but another idea." He does not deny that sensations in some way guide us or inform us of the qualities of physical objects, but they do so not by resembling the latter qualities. Nor is there any need for us to be aware of these sensations. Rather, it is just that we are naturally so built or so constituted that certain sensations tend to produce in us the strong, unavoidable conviction that objects with such-and-such qualities are present, even though there is nothing in common, no resemblance, between these sensations and the physical qualities.

This account marks a significant departure from the inclinations of other early modern philosophers. On this view, belief in external objects can be justified in a way that does not require that we possess some independent reason to think that our sensations can be trusted to inform us about these objects, or that we already be aware of the relevance of our sensations to the truth of our beliefs. Thus, Reid seems to have reacted to the epistemological problems of perception in early modern philosophy by embracing a form of what contemporary epistemologists call externalism about justified or rational belief. These beliefs can be justified foundationally, provided that we are naturally so constituted as to form such beliefs in response to our having these sensations.

1   Consider Locke's four reasons for thinking that our senses give us reliable information about the external world, especially the last of these four reasons—the argument from coherence and prediction. What would the external world skeptic say to challenge this argument?

2   Berkeley claims that the argument from perceptual relativity applies just as much to primary qualities as it does to secondary qualities. It was suggested in this chapter that an appeal to projective or perspectival geometry provides a response, at least for the properties of shape and size. Do you think this response is effective? Berkeley's argument and this response seem to assume that in our visual experiences we are primarily aware of two-dimensional images, though we interpret these as three-dimensional. Is this assumption correct, and can rejecting it provide an objection to the argument? Can an appeal to the other senses, like touch, help?

3   We sometimes have experiences in which our depth perception seems to shift without a change in our experience of colors or two-dimensional

features. For example, an ellipse drawn on a page might suddenly look like a circle or disc viewed at an angle; a circle with shading might look convex (like a sphere) or concave, or flip between these two possibilities. (Various visual illusions and geometric art, like the famous drawings of M. C. Escher, take advantage of these ambiguities in apparent depth perception.) Examine and reflect on these examples. Do they suggest that we are aware of three-dimensional properties of depth in experience? Do they raise a challenge to Berkeley's claim that we cannot separate or abstract the primary qualities of shape from qualities of color?

4 Consider introspection, reason, memory, and perception. Do you think Reid is right that no reason can be given for privileging one of these sources over the others? Can a Cartesian appeal to "clarity and distinctness" of at least some of the deliverances of reason, or introspection, help to block this concern, or would that just beg the question in some way?

Primary texts include Locke's *Essay Concerning Human Understanding* (1690): see Bk. II (Chs. i–ix) for his views on ideas acquired by sense, primary and secondary qualities, and perception; Bk. IV focuses on knowledge, and includes a discussion of our knowledge of the external world (Ch. xi). For Berkeley's critiques of Lockean and materialist views and defenses of idealism, see *Treatise Concerning the Principles of Human Knowledge* (1710) and *Three Dialogues between Hylas and Philonous* (1713). See Reid's *Inquiry into the Human Mind* (1764) and *Essays on the Intellectual Powers of Man* (1785), especially Essays II and VI, for his treatment of perception and his critique of the "way of ideas."

Bennett's "Substance, Reality, and Primary Qualities" (1965) is an excellent short article on Locke's views on the appearance/reality distinction and the primary/secondary quality distinction, including a defense of the latter against Berkeley's attack. For a more detailed and careful discussion of Locke on perception, the primary/secondary quality distinction, and connections to contemporary issues, see Mackie's *Problems from Locke* (1976).

For critical discussions of Reid's attack on the "way of ideas," see Lyons's *Perception and Basic Beliefs* (2009: 9–11) and Pust's "Skepticism, Reason, and Reidianism" (2013). For more on Reid's views on common sense and epistemology, see Nichols and Yaffe's entry on "Thomas Reid" in the *Stanford Encyclopedia of Philosophy* (2014).

3

Perceptual experience

This chapter provides an introduction to the main theories of perceptual or sensory experience: naïve realism, sense-datum theory, adverbialism, intentionalism, and a more recent view that might be understood as a more sophisticated version of naïve realism, metaphysical disjunctivism. In each case, we discuss the main motivations for the theory, the central principles they accept or deny, and some of the challenges and likely objections they face. The purpose is to introduce metaphysical problems of perception, lay some of the background necessary for the examination of epistemological theories that rely on assumptions regarding the nature of experience, and help avoid confusing epistemological and metaphysical issues.

It is not always clear what the early modern philosophers mean by "ideas," even in the context of discussing sensory experience. This is not to say that they had nothing to say about the nature of sensory experiences—in fact, we can trace the roots of a number of contemporary debates regarding the nature of sensory experience to the early modern philosophers. But rather than attempt to sort that out, we now turn to more recent debates regarding the nature of perceptual experience. In this chapter, we briefly discuss sense-datum theories, adverbial theories, intentional theories, and metaphysical disjunctivism, each successive theory motivated in part by the goal of avoiding difficulties with the preceding ones. These alternatives are not all mutually exclusive, though for the most part we focus on "pure" versions of each view.

There are two main objectives in discussing these views. The first is to introduce the reader to some metaphysical problems and theories concerned with perception, in part because some of the epistemological views discussed later in the book rely on assumptions about the nature of sensory experience. The second, related, objective is to help readers distinguish between metaphysical and epistemological theses, see connections between metaphysical and epistemological theses, but also guard against hastily drawing epistemological implications from metaphysical claims.

Naïve realism and the argument from hallucination

Traditional theories of perception, including the dominant view held by the early modern philosophers, are varieties of *indirect realism*. According to indirect realism, we are aware of or perceive external objects only in virtue of being directly aware of something else—our own ideas, sensations, mental states, sense data, appearances, etc. The *direct realist* denies this, claiming that we can be directly aware of external objects. As we shall see, there are different sorts of direct realists, since those who deny that we are aware of external objects by being aware of something else might still disagree about what it is to be aware of or perceive such objects.

It will be helpful to begin, though, with a view that is sometimes called *naïve realism*, according to which perception involves a direct awareness of the external object itself in such a way that one's experience literally involves or is constituted partly by that object. This is, in some ways, the most obvious alternative to indirect realism. The naïve realist might say: "In normal cases of perception you're aware of external objects and their features. That's just common sense. And you're not aware of them by being aware of mental states or anything like that (though you can be aware of those too). You're just aware of external objects directly. When you see them, they are part of your experience." This is sometimes called "naïve realism" because it is similar to what a philosophically unreflective subject might hold prior to, and perhaps even after, encountering the argument from the possibility of illusion and hallucination for the claim that we are never directly aware of such external objects. (We shall see that some defend rather sophisticated forms of "naïve realism," and have raised a number of objections to the argument from the possibility of hallucination.)

The naïve realist view accepts the existence of experiential or perceptual states, or state of awareness, that quite literally involve or are constituted by the external objects or qualities themselves. Genuine cases of perception involve an awareness of objects, and one would not count as being in the very same mental or experiential state if there were no such object. The traditional worry with this view is straightforward: it seems we could have the very same perceptual experiences in cases of hallucination that we have in genuine cases of perception, and if that is the case, then those experiences could not literally involve or be constituted partly by external objects. There's a parallel worry for mere illusions, where objects exist and may be perceived but do not have some quality or qualities that we experience them to have: it seems we could have the very same perceptual experiences in cases of illusion, so those experiences could not literally involve or be constituted partly by those external qualities. But so far, this claim comes very close to simply denying what the naïve realist is claiming. How do we motivate it? We can construct an argument against naïve realism by depending on the following two principles:

> The Indistinguishability Principle (IP): For any sensory experience of the sort that might be had in a genuine case of perception, it is possible to have an experience that is internally or subjectively indistinguishable from it, but in which there is no relevant physical object present (hallucination) or in which the physical object present lacks the property it appears to have (illusion).

> The Common Factor Principle (CFP): If perceptions, hallucinations, and illusions are internally or subjectively indistinguishable, then they have a sensory experience or sensory appearance in common, and the differences between the experiences, if any, are insignificant.

IP basically says that genuine, veridical perceptions are internally indistinguishable from certain hallucinations and illusions. IP is far less controversial than CFP. Hardly anyone would doubt that it is possible, in principle, to have an experience that one cannot distinguish subjectively or "from the inside" from an illusion or hallucination.

The CFP adds that if these are internally indistinguishable then the experiences involved must be the same kind, or have relatively insignificant differences. This principle can be motivated by asking the following question: Why is it that some perceptions, hallucinations, and illusions are internally or subjectively indistinguishable? Here's a plausible answer: what subjects experience in these cases, what they are conscious of or directly aware of, is exactly the same. That would account quite straightforwardly for why they cannot tell the difference between them. While there are stronger versions discussed in the literature under the same name, CFP does not say that the underlying experiences must be alike in all respects. Perhaps some indistinguishable experiences can be ever so slightly different; if our discriminatory abilities are limited we might not be able to detect these subtle differences. Even so, the general idea is clear enough: CFP claims that indistinguishable "good" (veridical) and "bad" (non-veridical) cases will involve experiences that are alike in significant, fundamental respects; any differences between them are relatively insignificant.

What follows from this? It follows that the indistinguishable "good" and "bad" cases share the same experiential or sensory state. But then, one's experience or sensory appearance in the perceptual case cannot be a form of awareness or experience that literally involves the external objects or events, because that would make these states significantly different from the sort of experience had in the indistinguishable cases of hallucination and illusion, where such objects or events are absent.

Let us consider a possible response to this argument that may help to clarify and further motivate CFP. The naïve realist might complain that it doesn't yet follow that we are not directly aware of external objects in cases of perception. We may grant in accordance with CFP that there is a sensory experience or appearance in common between a visual perception of a red bulgy tomato and an indistinguishable hallucination. But perhaps there is, in addition to that, an awareness of the red bulgy tomato when we see it that is not there in the case of hallucination. The problem is that it is difficult to square this with the internal indistinguishability of seeing and hallucinating a red bulgy tomato. If the awareness of the red bulgy tomato is really distinct from the sensory appearance that is in common, then I should be able to distinguish the two—it seems I would have to be, in a way, "seeing double" or having a double awareness when perceiving an actual tomato. In other words, if these cases really are indistinguishable, then they cannot involve such significantly different states of awareness. As we shall see, however, some "disjunctive" versions of naïve realism deny the claim of CFP so understood.

Sense-datum theory and the phenomenal principle

According to the sense-datum theory, in any case of genuine or veridical perception of a physical object, the subject is not directly aware of that object or any of its physical properties, but only of some non-physical or mind-dependent object, a "sense datum." Sense-datum theories are typically defended by appeal to a version of the argument from hallucination and/or illusion that employs the following principle:

> The Phenomenal Principle (PP): "If there sensibly appears to a subject to be something which possesses a particular sensible quality then there is something of which the subject is aware which does possess that sensible quality." (Robinson 1994: 32)

The sense-datum theorist accepts PP. The intuitive force of PP comes from the phenomenology of experience. Right now, there sensibly appears to be a bulgy red tomato in front of me, and it is very difficult for me to deny, while having this very experience, that I am aware of something that is bulgy and red. But what if I happen to be hallucinating? Even so, and even if I suspect or somehow know that I am hallucinating, it will still be just as difficult for me to deny that I am aware of something red and bulgy. But perhaps I could be aware of something red and bulgy without there actually being something red and bulgy here? That doesn't seem to make any sense, and doesn't capture my experience: the red and bulgy shape is right there before consciousness— how could I deny it? And how could I have a sensible appearance of redness and bulginess unless there really was something red and bulgy here? Could it be that I am aware of a *non-existent* red and bulgy shape? That sounds incoherent, and quite extravagant: how could there *be* non-existent objects?

It follows from IP, CFP, and PP that even in the "good" case of veridical, genuine perception of some object's having some sensible quality, there exists something that has that sensible quality, something other than the physical object. This object is the "sense datum," and a sensory appearance or sensation can be understood as an act of direct or immediate awareness of this sense datum. Sense-datum theory is thus typically understood as a kind of act-object theory, since it involves an act (or perhaps better, a relation) of awareness directed at an object, a sense datum.

Sense-datum theorists typically offer their view as part of an analysis of perception. It is in part in virtue of one's awareness of sense data that one can be aware of or perceive any physical object. Very roughly, S perceives an object O if and only if S is directly aware of a sense datum D, D resembles O in some central respects, and S's awareness of D is caused by O. We need to add that S's awareness of D must be caused in some appropriate, non-deviant way, for not just any causal process or relation will do. Suppose, for example, that I happen to eat the leaf of a plant that has hallucinogenic properties and, in fact, tends to cause people to hallucinate a plant just like it. My experience then satisfies the conditions above: the plant causes me to have an apparent perception of a plant just like it. But it doesn't cause the experience in the right way. We might try to avoid this problem by saying that S's awareness of D must be caused by O via the senses. But it's no small task filling out what "via the senses" means. If we want to allow for the possibility that very different animals and even aliens could perceive things, then we should not understand "via the senses" in terms of our sense organs or that of similar mammals. The causal relation must, it seems, be "appropriate" or "non-deviant," but it is notoriously difficult to analyze this without running into further counterexamples.

The sense-datum theory has largely, though not entirely, fallen out of favor, in part because it raises a number of puzzling questions that seem intractable.[1] When you are aware of a red and bulgy sense datum, *where* does this sense datum reside? Perhaps you will be tempted to say that it resides where the physical object resides, overlapping with it in physical space. But suppose you are hallucinating—does it reside there still? Or suppose you are looking at a square table from a particular perspective so that you are confronted with a rhombus-shaped sense datum. Where does that rhombus reside? Not on the surface of the table, for that is square. But where then? Are they literally in the mind? If the sense datum theorists don't want to claim that my mind or some part of it is literally square or rhomboid when I look at the table, or literally red and bulgy when I look at a tomato, they must apparently hold that there is a phenomenal space of some sort that is distinct from the mind. Moreover, wherever we put them, whether in a private, phenomenal space or a public, physical space, some further questions arise: Do these objects have only a momentary or continued existence? As I walk around a table do I experience one sense datum that changes its shape and size, or many different sense data over time? Could sense data exist even when we aren't aware of them, or have some features that we aren't aware of?

A particular objection related to the last of these questions can be put in the form of a dilemma. Consider the sort of experience you have upon looking at a speckled hen.[2] The sense-datum theorist seems committed to saying that your experience involves a speckled sense datum. Now, this sense datum has either a determinate or an indeterminate number of speckles. If it has a determinate number of speckles, the problem is that we might be unable to become aware of this determinate number, and this suggests that we are not directly aware of such sense data after all. On the other hand, if the number of speckles is indeterminate, then this seems to go against a plausible metaphysical principle that existing objects must be determinate: just as there can't be a hen that is speckled but lacks any determinate number of speckles, there can't be a sense datum that is speckled but lacks any determinate number of speckles.

Sense-datum theorists have attempted to give answers to some of these questions.[3] But many feel that the difficulty of answering them suggests that we have gone down the wrong path, and would rather not commit to the existence of such entities.

Sense-datum theory is sometimes also criticized for placing a "veil of perception" between us and physical objects, where this is taken to be objectionable either because it conflicts with common sense, leads to serious epistemological difficulties in responding to skepticism about the external world, or both.[4] However, as we shall see in more detail below, these concerns are far from decisive, and to the extent that there are serious problems here, the main traditional alternatives (adverbialism and intentionalism) face similar ones.

Adverbialism

In order to avoid the commitment to sense data, many who accept the common factor principle deny the phenomenal principle. There may sensibly appear to me to be an object with a particular sensible property, but that is compatible with there being no such object, physical or otherwise. There is a kind of experience that is in common between the perceptual and illusory cases, but this does not involve a direct awareness of a sense datum; there is no need for an act of awareness directed at some peculiar intermediary object. All the standard, traditional views accept that there must be some sort of causal connection between the external world object and one's sensory experience or sensory appearance in order for one to perceive the object. So, perhaps we can accept that there is some common factor between the good and bad cases, and also accept that in the good case in which a corresponding object exists and certain causal conditions obtain, the subject counts as perceiving that object. Thus, perhaps we can reject the phenomenal principle and avoid the indirect realist view that we are aware of objects in the external world only indirectly, by virtue of being directly aware of sense data, and thereby avoid the ontological commitments of the sense-datum theory.

 But what exactly is in common between the indistinguishable perceptual and illusory cases? What is it to have a sensory appearance as of an object having some property if it does not involve direct awareness of a sense datum that literally has that property? According to what is often called *adverbialism*, and sometimes *the theory of appearing*, rather than treat the apparently sensed property as a property of some object of which the subject is aware, we could treat it as *a way of sensing or experiencing* or *a way of being appeared to*.[5] Ducasse (1942) provides a helpful analogy: To dance a waltz is not to do something or perform some act—dancing—that takes something else—a waltz—as its object. Rather, it is a way or manner of dancing: dancing *waltzily*. The sentence "Pam dances a waltz" might thus be translated as "Pam dances waltzily." This may be linguistically awkward, but there is nothing incoherent about it, and it better captures the reality that we are dealing with a particular way of dancing rather than a dance directed at some object. Similarly, the sentence "Jude gave a loud cry" can be translated as "Jude cried loudly." Some sentences that have a subject-verb-noun structure, or a subject-verb-adjective-noun structure, can thus be expressed by sentences that have a subject-verb-adverb structure. The adverbialist gives the same treatment to the claim that I am experiencing red or having an appearance of red: this need not be understood as an act that takes some instance of red as its object, but rather just as a way of experiencing or being appeared to: experiencing *redly*, or being appeared to *redly*.

Can we really make sense of these adverbial constructions? Suppose I have a sensory appearance of a red square. What is it to be appeared to redly? What is it to be appeared to squarely? We can understand these terms either comparatively or non-comparatively. To understand experiencing (sensing, being appeared to, etc.) squarely in a comparative way is to take this to mean that I am having the sort of experience I normally would have in the presence of an object that is square. The problem with the comparative sense is that there seems to be no further explanation of the phenomenology—of what it is like to have the experience—that is in common between the internally indistinguishable cases. The comparative sense of being appeared to squarely is in a way an indirect characterization of the experience. It just tells me that I am having the sort of experience, whatever it is, that I would have when seeing something square. But that doesn't help me understand how it could seem or appear to me, *even in the hallucinatory case*, that there is something square. The account would fail to characterize the qualities or properties of my sensory experiences in any way that would illuminate why they count as appearances of objects of the relevant sort. The sense-datum theory at least had a straightforward response to that: you are directly aware of something that is literally square, that is red, and so on. The purely comparative characterization of experiences provides no such answer.

If we can at least sometimes understand these adverbial constructions in some non-comparative sense, offering a more direct characterization of the experience, then there might be room to make sense of the phenomenology. There are two potential problems here. First, there is a difficulty about how to understand something like "being appeared to squarely" in a non-comparative sense. What is it to be experiencing squarely? Or if we think of the qualities as applied to a state of experience as opposed to an act of experiencing, what is it for an experiential state (as opposed to some object) to have the quality of being square? Do these statements make any sense at all? Does anyone really understand what such statements amount to? It is intuitive that there are qualities of experience that determine or constitute what it is like to have these experiences—what philosophers often call "qualia". The worry is that while we might find it natural to think of experiences themselves being *painful*, having the quality of *pain*, or being constituted in part by such qualia, it is difficult to make any sense of experiences as *square* or occurring *squarely*. Perhaps there is some further characterization of such language possible, but that further characterization is what is important.

The second worry with the non-comparative characterization of experience is that, at least if the adverbialist hopes to account for the phenomenology of perceptual experience, it is no longer clear that adverbialism offers a direct realist alternative. We are appealing to some qualities of our own experiences to account for our having the same sensory appearance in the good and bad cases, explaining why it can seem to us that there is a red square here when there isn't. But then, in order for the adverbial view to help us account for how things seem to us, there apparently must be some sort of awareness or consciousness of these qualities.[6] If there is no awareness, but only a state with relevant qualities that is causally related in some "non-deviant" way to the external world, then it is not clear why we should regard this as amounting to any kind of perceptual *awareness* at all. So let us suppose that the adverbialist accepts the need for some consciousness or awareness of the qualities of experience that the adverbs refer to. Even setting aside the first worry above and granting that we can make sense of what these qualities are like, the view now seems to amount to an indirect theory of perception after all, with acts of awareness directed at our own states or their qualities rather than sense data. Perhaps the commitment to qualities of experience is not as worrisome as the commitment to sense data; but, on the other hand, the sense-datum theory doesn't have the first worry above, that of making sense of what it is to sense squarely.

But what exactly is the problem with saying we are directly aware of our mental states or their qualities as opposed to external-world objects? One complaint that is often used to motivate the theory we shall consider next, intentionalism, is that this view fails to accommodate the "transparency" of perceptual experience (Harman 1990). Consider your current surroundings. In my case, I am surrounded by some items of furniture, books, windows, and trees nearby. I also see that it is a dark and rainy day. Phenomenologically, my perceptual experiences involve an awareness of the external world—of these objects, their properties, and events happening around me. I can also introspect and ask myself what my current perceptual experiences are like. According to the claim of transparency, when we do this we only become aware of these external objects and events, and their relations to each other (including our own bodies). There seem to be no intrinsic qualities of experience, no qualia to fix on. Our experiences are, so to speak, "transparent," in that introspection reveals nothing intrinsic to them. Upon introspecting I may become aware that I am having experiences of furniture, books, trees, and so on, but my awareness involves no intrinsic "qualia". Perceptual experiences are thus "transparent" or "diaphanous," revealing only what the external objects are like, not any intrinsic qualities of the experiences themselves. The adverbialist who offers a qualitative, non-comparative analysis of sensing or appearing states must apparently deny this claim of transparency.

Intentionalism

The defining feature of intentional theories of perceptual experience is that they take perceptual experiences to have "intentional" or representational content. That is, they take them to have "content" not in the sense that a drawer or box can have content, but in the sense that a speech or book can. For an experience to have content in the latter sense is for it to have something that is *assessable for accuracy or truth*, and so have what we might call *accuracy conditions*, conditions under which the experience would be accurate, just as there are conditions under which the assertions made in a speech or book would be accurate.[7]

It is helpful to compare this with the standard view of belief. Beliefs are *propositional attitudes*: they involve a subject's standing in some relation to a *proposition*, and in particular having an attitude of *belief* toward some *proposition*, where a proposition is an abstract entity that has truth value or that can be true or false. A proposition is thus assessable for accuracy or truth and so the belief, too, is derivatively assessable for truth. For example, my belief that there is a cat on the bed involves my having a particular sort of attitude towards the proposition <a cat is on the bed>, and the belief is true just in case the proposition is true—just in case there in fact is a cat on the bed. The intentionalist takes perceptual experiences to similarly involve one's standing in some relation to, or having a state with, some representation or proposition, something assessable for accuracy or truth; and the experience itself is also derivatively assessable for accuracy or truth. (Some philosophers might take there to be kinds of representational content that are not propositional, but for our purposes we can take propositional and representational contents to be the same sort of thing.) For example, if there visually appears to me to be a cat on the bed, then the content of my experience is accurate, and so the experience is accurate, just in case there is indeed a cat on the bed. This state is like a belief in being "non-factive": just as one may believe that P even while P is false, it may visually or perceptually seem to me that P even while P is false. But experiencing is not the same as believing; I might, after all, suspect that I am the victim of an illusion or hallucination and withhold belief, but continue to have an experience with the same content. One important difference between a perceptual experience and attitudes like belief is that the former aren't just representational but also *presentational*: *they present the world as being a certain way*.

It is worth repeating that the views we are considering are not all mutually exclusive, and we have been focusing on "pure" forms of each for simplicity. In particular, some might accept adverbialism, the sense-datum theory, or naïve realism, while also accepting intentionalism; there is nothing about these views that *trivially* rules out that perceptual experiences have representational or propositional content. While intentionalism is a very popular view, it remains controversial. A number of philosophers have thought, and some continue to hold, that while a perceptual experience may be associated with certain contents, or tend to give rise to certain judgments, guiding us to believe truths and sometimes misleading us to believe things that are false, strictly speaking the experiences themselves have no contents. They might hold that sensory or perceptual experiences are states of being appeared to, have phenomenal qualities or "raw feels," or involve our standing in some relation to sense data or to the external world, *and* deny that these states are the sorts of things that are themselves accurate or inaccurate, true or false.[8]

Intentionalists typically hold that there is a common factor between the good and bad cases: an intentional state. Since this state is non-factive, intentionalists can deny the phenomenal principle: a perceptual appearance of something having a particular property involves an appearance *that* it has the property, but since the latter proposition could be false, there need not be any such object. In other words, apparently perceived properties are *represented*, but not necessarily *instantiated*.

Part of the motivation of intentionalism is that it avoids the commitment to sense data, while also improving on adverbialism's attempt to accept the common factor principle and account for the indistinguishability of the good and bad cases. As just discussed, there is a related motivation for intentionalism, which is that it preserves the "transparency" of perceptual experience. Some intentionalists might allow that we can be aware of qualia in some cases, but still accept a transparency claim when it comes to the primary sorts of perceptual experiences we have. Thus, while some might claim that pain is a qualitative feature of our own experiences, shapes and colors are not—they are features of objects out there in the world.

This does, however, raise a problem for the intentionalist. For if the intentionalist accepts the common factor principle, and claims that in cases of seeing or perceiving we are aware of the properties of external *objects* rather than properties of *experience*, then we must apparently accept that in the internally or phenomenologically indistinguishable cases of hallucination or illusion, we are also aware of properties of external objects rather than of experience. But in bad or illusory cases, there is no such external object present. The claim of transparency thus seems to conflict with the common factor principle. Indeed, it seems that the sense-datum theory does better here: it can preserve the sense that we are transparently aware of objects with properties, and allow for these same objects to be present in the bad cases as well! The sense-datum theorist might thus claim to have a significant advantage over intentionalism and adverbialism.

How might the intentionalist respond? The intentionalist might claim that there is still something in common in the good and bad cases: there is the same intentional state, and so the same sorts of objects are represented as existing; the same properties are represented as instantiated by the existing objects. In the good case, the represented objects actually exist, and the represented properties are instantiated; in the bad case, they are not. One might still reasonably worry, however, about how to square this with the initial claim of transparency. Recall that the claim of transparency was that we are aware of the objects themselves, not of our experiences or experiential properties. But again, in the bad case the represented object does not exist. If we are not aware of sense data or qualia, what is it that we are aware of? Should we say that we are aware of a *non-existent* object? That seems to make no sense. Should we say that we only *seem* to be aware of such objects and properties, but actually we are not? That would just raise the question of what it is we *are* aware of in such cases. Should we say that there is no awareness at all? That fails to take seriously the phenomenology of illusions and hallucinations; even when I suspect I am hallucinating a tomato or seeing it but having an illusion that it is red, I can ask: "If *this* is not really a tomato, what is it? If *this* is not the tomato's color, what is it?"[9]

Before moving on to consider disjunctivism, we should distinguish here between at least two theories about the nature of contents. According to one sort of view, often called the Russellian[10] theory, or the singular content theory, a proposition is partly constituted by particular objects, properties, relations, etc. For example, the proposition expressed by "Lulu the cat is grey" is partly constituted by Lulu herself, that particular cat, the property of being a cat, and the property of greyness.

There are a number of views of the nature of content that would reject this, including views that identify propositions with Fregean "manners of presentation." In the philosophy of language, the Fregean view of contents can be motivated by appeal to the cognitive difference between sentence pairs like "Hesperus is the morning star" and "Hesperus is the evening star." Someone might assert, accept, or believe one of these while denying or leaving open whether the other is true, even though "the morning star" and "the evening star" are in fact, unbeknownst to the subject, the very same celestial body (Venus). Fregeans argue that the two sentences must have the same truth values but can clearly differ in the role they play in the subject's thinking and reasoning, and so, even though the descriptions refer to or denote the same things they must involve different "modes of presentation." Fregean views of content can be motivated in a similar way, by considering cases in which subjects seem to experience the same things but in different ways. For example, I might continue to have an experience of Lulu the cat as *small* and *grey* even though there are quite significant changes in my experience as the lighting conditions and my distance from Lulu change. (The sense-datum theorists sometimes appeal to these sorts of variations in experience of stable physical objects to motivate their view of sense data.) The Fregean claims that there is a kind of size and color constancy in my experiences in this case, though the same size and color can have varying "modes of presentation." The Fregean thus attempts to separate and make sense of the varying and constant features without positing something like sense data.[11]

While there are other views, including hybrid views that allow for both Russellian and Fregean contents (perhaps because they serve different purposes or are needed to handle different cases), for our purposes we can distinguish Russellian contents from Fregean and other non-Russellian contents that are *not* constituted by the particular objects and properties that the terms of the corresponding sentences refer to; they may involve modes of presentation, or other abstract or conceptual items that *refer* to such objects and properties, but are not themselves constituted by these very objects and properties.

What is the motivation for taking some contents, at least perceptual ones, to be singular or Russellian in the specific sense of involving external objects as constituents? The intuitive idea is that genuine cases of perception have a particular rather than general or abstract content. When I perceive a cat's being on a bed, my perception is not merely that there is a cat on a bed but that *that* particular cat is on *that* particular bed. The view that perceptions involve singular contents accommodates this intuition. It may help to compare this to cases of *veridical hallucination*. Suppose that I actually see my bed, but hallucinate a cat on it. Suppose there also happens to be a cat on the bed exactly where I hallucinate there to be one, though I don't see it because the hallucination takes over that part of my visual field. The proposition that there is a cat on that bed is true. But this would not be enough to make my experience be about *that* cat. The experience might be internally indistinguishable from a genuine perception, but on the "Russellian" view that we are considering, there is some content—Russellian content—that is different.

The attentive reader may have noticed that on the view that there are at least some such Russellian contents, the perceptual and internally indistinguishable hallucinatory experiences can have different contents, and so this view denies that there is a common underlying intentional state. As we shall see, some (though not all) disjunctivists might thus accept a kind of intentionalism and hold that one might have an internally indistinguishable hallucination of there being a cat on a bed, but the particularity or singularity of the experience would be merely illusory.

Metaphysical disjunctivism

The concerns expressed toward the end of the last section might lead one to reconsider the common factor principle. Perhaps internally indistinguishable experiences can involve different—radically different—experiences. That is, indeed, what metaphysical disjunctivism claims: indistinguishable cases of perception and hallucination involve significantly, fundamentally different sorts of experiences. This leaves open that they have some things in common, or even that they are significantly alike.

A natural objection to a strong version of the common factor principle that says the underlying experiences must be exactly alike is that our abilities to discriminate between experiences are limited; some differences in our appearances or sensory experiences outstrip our discriminatory abilities, even in ideal circumstances. Indeed, some have offered powerful arguments to think that we cannot always discriminate between experiences that are phenomenally different. Consider, for example, the experience of very similar colors A, B, and C, where one can tell the difference between A and C, but where each pair A and B, and B and C, are indistinguishable. A natural expla-nation of this phenomenon is that they are each phenomenally different, but the nearby shades are internally indistinguishable.[12] Traditional accounts can allow that *some* indistinguishable perceptions and hallucinations are different in these subtle ways.

Metaphysical disjunctivism is more radical: it treats all indistinguishable cases of perception and hallucination as significantly and fundamentally different kinds of experience or mental state. This also explains the label for the view. Disjunctivists will agree that there can seem or appear to me to be a tomato on the table whether I am perceiving or hallucinating; but they will understand its seeming to me that there is a tomato on the table to mean that I am *either* seeing a tomato *or* hallucinating a tomato. They thus offer a *disjunctive* analysis of sensory seemings or appearances.

One central motivation for metaphysical disjunctivism is that it preserves the direct or "naïve" realist view discussed earlier in the chapter: the disjunc-tivist can treat seeing as a transparent, direct awareness of the external world. Moreover, since it rejects the common factor principle, it denies that hallucinations involve the same basic sort of awareness, and so it can avoid the problems with the simple naïve realist and intentionalist views discussed above. The disjunctive analysis of appearances allows one to say that things can "appear the same" in perceptual and hallucinatory cases, but that is really just to say that perceptions and hallucinations can be internally indistinguishable.

We will evaluate the disjunctivist's rejection of the common factor principle presently. But first, let us briefly consider *the causal argument* against naïve realism, in order to see how a disjunctivist version of the view would reply. Our perceptual experiences are the effects of external world objects on our organs and peripheral neural states. The same causes have the same effects. So, if we produce the same neural states in the absence of the external world objects, then we would produce the very same experiences. But then, we could produce the very same perceptual experiences even when the external objects are absent by stimulating the peripheral nervous system. For example, I could be made to have the very same experience that I would have in a case of perceiving a tomato without the presence of the tomato. But according to naïve realism, these experiences cannot exist without the existence of the relevant external objects, since they involve a direct awareness of the objects themselves. So, naïve realism is false.

The naïve realist might respond by denying that the act of awareness involved in perception is a mere effect of the stimulation of the nervous system. The relevant act of awareness and the act of seeing are one and the same, an act that is constituted by the entire causal process. As one proponent of naïve realism puts it: "Seeing goes all the way out to the things seen"; seeing and hallucinating are thus "distinctively different acts of awareness ... individuated by different objects of awareness" (Johnston 2004: 139).

One of the most significant problems for disjunctivism concerns the explanation of indistinguishability. Given that some perceptions are indistinguishable from hallucinations, what accounts for this indistinguishability? If the experiences are significantly different in kind, why are they indistinguishable? The disjunctivist might be tempted to say that objects can be indistinguishable by sight despite being radically different, like zebras and cleverly disguised mules, real and plastic fruit, and so on. Why can't experiences be similarly indistinguishable by introspection? But, intuitively, experiences are as they appear, whereas external objects need not be (Hellie 2007). And it seems that I can learn what it is like to *perceive* something even if I am hallucinating—e.g., what it is like to perceive something red or square, even if I don't see and never have seen anything that is red or square. How could this be, if there were not something in common between hallucinations and perceptions? It is thus natural to think that internally indistinguishable perceptions and hallucinations do have something in common, whether it is some phenomenal or qualitative character, or intentional content, or both.

So, we need some reason to think that different experiences can be internally or introspectively indistinguishable. The disjunctivist might point out that it is a substantive, non-trivial claim that we have the ability to discriminate experiences that have different qualitative or intentional properties. As we have seen, there is some reason to think that indistinguishable experiences can be different. However, those reasons at best support the indistinguishability of subtle changes in phenomenal character, for qualities that fall on a continuum, like slight changes in color or temperature. That hardly warrants thinking that experiences that have radically different qualitative or representational features can be internally indistinguishable. Perhaps the disjunctivist can say something about the content or the phenomenal character of hallucinations that would help.

Let us distinguish between *negative disjunctivism* and *postive disjunctivism*. According to negative *disjunctivism* we can only say that hallucinations are experiences that are not perceptions but are internally indistinguishable from them. To hallucinate a cat is to have an experience that is internally indistinguishable from a visual perception of a cat, but where no such cat is perceived. (This might remind the reader of the merely comparative adverbialist treatment of sense appearances: to experience cat-ly is to have just the sort of experience one normally would have in the presence of a cat.) The main worry with the negative disjunctivist characterization of hallucination is that it fails to provide any illuminating explanation for internal indistinguishability.[13] Relatedly, it doesn't seem to help us understand why we would still seem to experience particulars even though our hallucinatory contents lack particularity.

According to *positive disjunctivism*, there is something positive we can say about hallucinations. One might, for example, claim that in the hallucinatory case we are aware of sense data or qualia, and not aware of the external objects. This could be understood as a version of naïve realism, where our experiences or states of awareness are constituted in part by external objects in the case of perception but by sense data or qualia in the case of hallucination. It could also be understood as a version of disjunctivism about content if, for example, we take experiences to have propositional contents constituted by external objects in cases of perception, but by sense data or qualia in cases of hallucination. And perhaps the awareness of qualia, or of sense data, can help explain the internal indistinguishability—after all, at least when it comes to sense data, these have qualities like color and shape despite being essentially different, mind-dependent objects. Perhaps they can be indistinguishable from physical objects. Moreover, there need not be an illusion of particularity—it's just that different sorts of particulars are present in the case of hallucination as compared with perception.

Perhaps the most serious problem for positive disjunctivism is the screening-off problem (Martin 2004). This problem is similar to the causal argument against naïve realism we considered above; it could be considered an extension of that argument, directed specifically at the positive disjunctivist. Consider the disjunctivist who says that in the hallucinatory case we are aware of a sense datum. In the case of a hallucination of a cat on my bed, the explanation of this hallucination is presumably that there is a complex neural event or process that causes me to be aware of the relevant sense data. But now consider the case of an internally indistinguishable perception of a cat on my bed. This too surely involves a similar neural event or process, one that would therefore cause me to be aware of the sense datum in the perceptual case as well. Not only do we seem to have a significant common factor between the two cases, but the awareness of the sense datum in the case of genuine perception suffices to explain why I seem to perceive a cat on my bed. There is no need, then, to appeal to an experience that is partly constituted by or involves the external object itself in order to explain how things seem in the veridical case, since awareness of sense data is sufficient. The awareness of sense data "screens off" the explanation of how things seem to us that appeals to awareness of external objects.

It might be thought that the disjunctivist can just deny that there is any awareness of sense data in the veridical case. But that seems highly implausible, for why isn't the same neural activity sufficient for one to experience a sense datum in the case of perception if it is sufficient in the case of hallucination? It is implausible to suggest that one's brain state somehow detects how it is being produced and blocks the production of the sense datum, or that the external object blocks production of the sense datum by some action at a distance (Robinson 1994: 153–4).

Perhaps the best response that a positive disjunctivist can give is to deny that we are aware of the same thing in perceptual and hallucinatory cases, but depart from a simple disjunctivist view by allowing that what we are aware of can overlap in some significant way. One of the more sophisticated views of this sort is defended by Mark Johnston (2004). According to this view, the common factor in internally indistinguishable cases is a "sensible profile," which is a complex, partly qualitative and partly relational property. To take a simple case: if I look at the sun or a bright light and then shift my focus onto a white wall, I might be aware of a sensible profile, a complex property—roughly, the property of *being-yellow-and-circular-and-in-front-of-me-now*. (The "*in-front-of-me-now*" part is the spatiotemporal relational part of the complex; the "*yellow-and-circular*" part is the qualitative part of the complex.) I am not aware of an instance of this property, since there is no yellow circle in front of me now. And even if there were a yellow circle because I accidentally happened to focus on a spot on the wall that had one (a case of veridical hallucination), I would still not be aware of that yellow circle, but only of the complex property. More generally: In the case of hallucination I am aware only of the sensible profile, consisting of properties and relations. These properties and relations are not instantiated, not had by any particulars. In the case of an indistinguishable perception these qualities and relations are instantiated, and I am aware of the *instantiated* sensible profile. In the case of a veridical hallucination the qualities and relations are instantiated, but I am only aware of the profile and not of its instantiation.

One might be tempted to claim that in the veridical case I am aware of the yellow circle indirectly, in virtue of being aware of the sensible profile. That is not Johnston's view. On his view, as I understand it, I am aware of *more* in the case of perception than I am in the illusory case, but the awareness remains direct: I am aware of an *instantiation of a* sensory profile, and not merely of a sensory profile that happens to be instantiated. I am aware of particulars having certain properties and standing in certain relations; in the hallucinatory case I am aware only of a sensory profile.

Notice that this account preserves the transparency claim while avoiding problems we raised above with simple naïve realist and intentionalist views: there is no need to say that we are aware of non-existent objects, or lack any awareness, in hallucinatory cases. We are aware of abstract entities, uninstantiated properties and relations, but not non-existent ones. We also avoid commitment to sense data understood as objects that have or instantiate these properties and relations. Sensible profiles can mimic or strongly suggest particularity and instantiation. When I hallucinate a bird flying through the air, it may seem that it must be a particular, because only particulars have motion—properties do not. But sensible profiles can mimic particularity, or strike us as moving particulars.

Let us return now to the screening-off problem. Does Johnston avoid this problem? It might seem that he does: in the case of (non-veridical) hallucination, one is aware of an uninstantiated sensory profile; in the case of veridical hallucination, one is aware of a sensory profile that happens to be instantiated, but not of the instantiation; in a case of perception, one is aware of an instantiation of a sensory profile. So, there is no need to think of the case of perception as involving an awareness of an uninstantiated sensory profile in addition to an awareness of its instantiation, and so one's awareness does explain how things seem in the veridical case. However, some worry that on this interpretation of Johnston's view the screening-off problem remains (Fish 2010: 99–100). For if an awareness of an uninstantiated sensible profile results from a neural event in the case of a hallucination, why should it not result from a neural event in the case of a perception? The awareness of the uninstantiated, abstract sensory profile would "screen off" the explanation of how things seem to us that appeals to awareness of the instantiation of a sensory profile.

Replacing sense data with sensible profiles

We discussed above a number of prominent theories regarding the nature of perception and perceptual experiences, ending with a discussion of metaphysical disjunctivism. I would like to conclude by mentioning one more possible theory that, like Johnston's view, accepts that we can be aware of something like abstract "sensible profiles," but that is not a direct or naïve realist theory of perception. Suppose we accept that we are directly aware of sensible profiles, but not of their instantiations or the concrete objects that instantiate them; we are at best indirectly aware of the latter. This is the view essentially defended by Peter Forrest (2005). On this view, we can accept the common factor principle, while also accepting that awareness does connect us with something real—though abstract. This seems to preserve the advantages over sense-datum theory, adverbialism and (non-disjunctive) intentionalism that Johnston's view seems to have. Is this view preferable to Johnston's? That may depend in part on whether Johnston is right that his view is able to avoid the screening-off problem, and on other considerations in favor of being an indirect realist as opposed to a naïve or direct realist about external objects.

From metaphysics to epistemology

Some may jump on the naïve-realist bandwagon on the grounds that it solves epistemological problems. But a word of caution is in order here: nothing follows immediately or trivially about whether we have epistemic justification or knowledge about the external world from the view that we can be directly aware of or acquainted with external objects. We would need to know more about what our knowledge or justification depends on, and how such acts of awareness can make a difference to justification, especially when, as is the case even on the disjunctivist view, there seems to be a sense in which we cannot tell "from the inside" whether we are in a good case of perception or a bad case of hallucination.

This point about the connections between metaphysical and epistemological problems applies more generally. The competing views discussed in this chapter have no epistemological conclusions without *epistemic principles* connecting experience or perception to justification or knowledge. An account of how, or in virtue of what, an experience or perception can provide anything like evidence, reason, or justification for a perceptual belief is still needed. Moreover, even if some forms of adverbialism or intentionalism can claim that sensory experiences are *vehicles* of sensory awareness and need not themselves be *objects* of awareness, these vehicles could still, so to speak, fail to reach their destinations, and even if they reach them, is it or is it not relevant that we may not be able to tell that they do? So the epistemological benefits of these alternatives to sense-datum theory should not be exaggerated. None of this is to deny that there can be important connections between metaphysics and epistemology, but only that more care needs to be taken to discover them.[14]

1   Suppose you are presently having a very vivid hallucination of this book. Ask yourself the following questions, and note your intuitive responses. Are you in a state that involves some sort of awareness of something or other? Is there something *of which* you are aware? Does this something *exist*? Does it share any of the qualities of a real book? If not, what could it be?

2   Place a pencil in half a glass of water and notice how, from certain angles, it looks bent, broken, or crooked. Ask yourself the following questions, and note your intuitive responses. Are you aware of something that is bent, broken, or crooked? If so, what are you aware of? Is it something that *exists*? Does it share any qualities with a real pencil? If not, what could it be?

3   Intentionalists sometimes object to the phenomenal principle by noting that various representational or intentional states don't entail the existence of the objects they represent or are about. For example, I may intend to search for bigfoot, ghosts, witches, or the fountain of youth, and even believe that the object of my search exists, but none of this implies that it does. Can't the same be true of apparent perceptions— can't I have them without there being anything, whether physical or mind-dependent, that has the qualities I apparently perceive? How do you think the sense-datum theorist would respond? Is there some dis-analogy here, or something special about perceptual experiences in contrast to things like intentions and beliefs?

4   A good counterfeit can be physically indistinguishable from the real thing, but that wouldn't make it the real thing. For example, consider the official currency of a country. There is something about the manner in which such items are produced, or about their source, that makes them different, so that an item that does not have this sort of source would not count as the real thing. Does this analogy help the disjunctivist's case for the claim that although the same physical brain states can be produced in the head in genuine perceptions and hallucinations, the experiences are importantly different? Are there important respects in which these are dis-analogous?

Fish's *Philosophy of Perception* (2010) is one of the best introductions to the philosophy of perception available, with whole chapters devoted to sense-datum theories, adverbialism, intentionalism, disjunctivism, analyses of perception, and more. Swartz's *Perceiving, Sensing, and Knowing* (1965) is an old but excellent collection, with many highly influential works on the analysis of perception, sense-datum and adverbial theory, and perceptual knowledge.

For detailed (and at least partial) defenses of sense-datum theory, see Price's *Perception* (1932), Jackson's *Perception: A Representative Theory* (1977), and Robinson's *Perception* (1994). An earlier, classical defense of sense-datum theory is given by Russell in *The Problems of Philosophy* (1912). For a classical critique of sense-datum theory, see Barnes's "The Myth of Sense Data" in the Swartz volume (1965). For a recent critique that focuses on the question "where are sense data located?" see Huemer's *Skepticism and the Veil of Perception* (2001: Ch. 7).

For early developments of adverbialism, see Ducasse, "Moore's 'Refutation of Idealism'" (1942) and Chisholm, *Perceiving: A Philosophical Study* (1957). For critiques, see Jackson's "On the Adverbial Analysis of Visual Experience" (1975), and Butchvarov's "The Adverbial Theories of Consciousness" (1980). Tye defends adverbialism against Jackson's critique in "The Adverbial Theory: A Defense of Sellars against Jackson" (1975). For a more recent defense, see Paul Coates's *The Metaphysics of Perception* (2007).

Early developments of intentionalism took the form of theories that analyzed experience in terms of beliefs or belief acquisition (e.g., Armstrong 1961 and 1968; Pitcher 1971), but most intentionalists reject the belief-acquisition theory. Martin's "Perceptual Content" (1994) and Siegel's "The Contents of Perception" in the *Stanford Encyclopedia of Philosophy* provide excellent introductions to intentionalism and theories of perceptual content. Harman's "The Intrinsic Quality of Experience" (1990) defends intentionalism and the transparency thesis. For recent critiques of intentionalism, see Robinson's *Perception* (1994; also includes a discussion of intentionality in early modern philosophy), and Travis's (2004) "The Silence of the Senses." For defenses, see Byrne's "Experience and Content" (2009), Pautz's "Why Explain Visual Experience in Terms of Content" (2010), and Siegel's "Do Experiences Have Contents?" (2010a), and her book *The Contents of Visual Experience* (2010b), which also discusses what contents our visual experiences have, and argues that the contents can be quite rich.

For a very good entry and selection of resources, see Fish's "Disjunctivism" in the *Internet Encyclopedia of Philosophy*. Byrne and Logue's "Either/Or" (2008) provides a very good introduction to disjunctivism, and the two anthologies on *Disjunctivism* by Haddock and Macpherson (2008) and Byrne and Logue (2009) contain essential readings on the topic. Johnston's "The Obscure Objects of Visual Hallucination" (2004) is a long but rewarding discussion of the argument from hallucination and disjunctivism.

For useful discussions regarding the connection (or lack thereof) between metaphysical direct/indirect realism and epistemological direct/indirect realism, see BonJour's entry on "Epistemological Problems of Perception" in the *Stanford Encyclopedia of Philosophy*, and Lyons's *Perception and Basic Beliefs* (2009: 8–14).

4

An introduction to contemporary epistemology

The chapter introduces some central controversies in epistemology and related epistemic concepts and distinctions. We begin the chapter with a discussion of the traditional analysis of knowledge as true justified belief, the famous Gettier problem for the traditional analysis, and some attempts to modify the traditional analysis in response to the problem. We also discuss, very briefly, the question of whether knowledge requires certainty. The chapter then elaborates on two central questions in epistemology (What is the nature of justification and knowledge? How much of it do we have?) and their relation to the traditional epistemologist's preoccupation with skepticism. The regress argument for foundationalism is introduced, as well as the internalist-externalist controversy and the distinction between mental state foundationalism and external world foundationalism.

A traditional analysis of knowledge

The main goal of this chapter is to introduce the reader to some central questions and controversies in contemporary epistemology, and to some key epistemic concepts and distinctions. Let us begin by considering the traditional analysis of knowledge.

According to a traditional analysis or conception of knowledge, arguably *the* traditional analysis of knowledge, one has knowledge that *P* if and only if one has a *justified* and *true belief* that *P*. That is, the following three conditions are each necessary and together sufficient for *S* to know that *P* at time *t*:

1 *S* believes that *P* at *t*.

2 *P* is true.

3 *S* is justified in believing that *P* at *t*.

Let's call this the "JTB" (justified true belief) analysis or conception of *knowledge*. The belief condition (1) is intuitively obvious. One cannot know that *P* without believing that *P*, where a belief is a positive attitude of accepting or assenting to, rather than doubting, questioning, or denying *P*. The paradigm case of belief is that of making an explicit judgment, a conscious or active belief that *P*—what philosophers often call an *occurrent* belief. But, from a commonsense perspective, I know or at least believe much more than what I explicitly or consciously believe: I already believe, for example, that coffee mugs, cats, and birds exist, that Paris is the capital of France, that I have three children, that I have two hands, and so on; and if knowledge requires belief and I do indeed know these things then I must already believe them. For each of the latter propositions, at some point in the past I thought explicitly about and came to accept it, and I thereby acquired the disposition to consciously accept or assent to the proposition again upon considering it. In something like this sense, I continue to believe it. At any one time, at most only a few of my beliefs are occurrent—explicitly thought, considered, or used in deliberation—and all the others are "stored" or merely dispositional. (This is a rough characterization of the distinction between occurrent and non-occurrent, merely dispositional beliefs, but it will do for our purposes.)

(2) is also intuitively obvious. Suppose I claim to know that there is a café around the corner. If you tell me that the café actually just went out of business, then I would conclude that I *thought* I knew (and perhaps at one point did know) that there was a café around the corner, but since it is no longer true I do not now know it. We shall assume, here and throughout the book, that a "correspondence theory of truth" is correct. Roughly, for a proposition to be true is for it to correspond to reality, or for the world to be as the proposition says it is.

The first two conditions are not sufficient for knowledge. A belief might be based on little more than a wild guess or wishful thinking, or result from one's being knocked on the head, and yet it might be true. Or, more realistically, it might be the product of confused, fallacious reasoning, and yet be true. Intuitively, such a belief would not count as knowledge. Something seems to be missing in these cases, and present in genuine cases of knowledge. What is it? In such cases the subject is not *justified* in believing the proposition in question. More specifically, the subject is not *epistemically* justified, even if the subject is justified in some pragmatic or moral sense. In order for one's belief to be *epistemically* justified, one must have a reason or evidence to think that the proposition believed is *true*. Perhaps the subject who is knocked on the head, or who reasons fallaciously, is not violating any norms of morality or prudence; the subject may yet fail to have any good evidence, reason, or justification in favor of the truth of the proposition. On the traditional view, the possession of justification involves the possession of evidence or reasons in favor of the truth of one's belief, though as we shall see, some contemporary accounts (most clearly, "externalist" ones) deny that epistemic justification always requires possession of a reason in favor of the truth of one's belief.

This is not to deny that there are contexts in which it is natural to say that someone "knows" that P when they have only a true belief that P. For example, I might ask a group of people what the capital of Bahrain is, and regard everyone who correctly believes it to be Manama to "know" that the capital of Bahrain is Manama, whether or not they have good evidence for believing this. But that is not what I have in mind in most cases, and is not particularly interesting.

Almost all contemporary epistemologists have given up the JTB analysis of knowledge, with the "Gettier problem" being perhaps the main reason for this. Though Bertrand Russell raised a similar problem much earlier (1912), it was made explicit and popularized by Edmund Gettier in the early 1960s. Suppose that we accept the following assumptions. First, it is possible to be epistemically justified in believing a proposition that is in fact false. I might have excellent reasons to believe something—good enough to justify my belief—and yet it might turn out that what I believe is false. Second, for any proposition P, if S is justified in believing P, and S competently deduces Q from P and accepts Q as a result, then S is justified in believing Q. Third, the degree of justification required for knowledge does not entail or guarantee truth. While the Cartesian conception of knowledge could arguably be inter-preted as a kind of JTB analysis, it rejects this last assumption, and is not vulnerable to the Gettier problem. However, most contemporary epistemolo-gists hold that the third assumption is correct: I can know, for example, that my car is in the driveway where I left it, that Paris is the capital of France, and that I have hands, even though my justification for each fails to guarantee the truth or rule out the possibility of error. Let us grant these assumptions for now.

Gettier challenged the traditional analysis of knowledge by presenting cases in which the three conditions are satisfied and yet, intuitively, the subject does not know the relevant proposition. Here are Gettier's (1963) two cases:

Case 1: Smith believes on good evidence—good enough for justification—that *Jones is the man who will get the job*, and that *Jones has ten coins in his pocket*. On this basis, he infers that *the man who will get the job has ten coins in his pocket*. However, what Smith does not know is that *he* is actually going to be offered the job, and he happens to have ten coins in his pocket. So, Smith has a justified *and true* belief that the man who will get the job has ten coins in his pocket. But, intuitively, this does not count as knowledge.

Case 2: Smith has very good evidence that *Jones owns a Ford*. He infers from this the disjunction that *either Jones owns a Ford or Brown is in Barcelona*. As it so happens, he's wrong about Jones—he doesn't own a Ford—and right about Brown—Brown is in Barcelona. So his inferred belief is true and justified. But, intuitively, it is not knowledge.

Here is a third example, from Bertrand Russell (1912: Ch. 13). Though Russell presents it as an argument against defining knowledge as true belief, we can also use it against the JTB analysis:

Case 3: Smith believes that *the late Prime Minister's name is Balfour*, and believes this on the basis of good, justifying evidence. Smith infers on the basis of this that *the late Prime Minister's name begins with a 'B'*. The latter belief is true, but only because the late Prime Minister's name is Bannerman. The belief is true and justified, but intuitively not knowledge.

Notice that the examples all have a similar structure: Smith forms a false justified belief (that Jones is the man who will get the job, that Jones owns a Ford, that the late Prime Minister's name is Balfour) and competently infers another belief from it, a belief that happens to be true.

One thing to notice is that in each case the truth of the belief is in some intuitive sense merely accidental. The belief does turn out to be true, but its truth is not related in the right sort of way to the subject's ultimate reason or evidence for holding the belief. We might try to use this idea to amend the analysis: S knows that P if and only if:

1 S believes that P at t.

2 P is true.

3 S is justified in believing that P at t.

4 P's truth is not merely *accidentally* related to S's justification for believing that P at t.

Since the above cases all fail to satisfy condition (4), they do not count as knowledge according to this analysis. While this is intuitively correct, the problem is that no matter how strong a justification one has, short of certainty, it remains to some degree a matter of *luck* or *accident* that one's belief is true. So, assuming that the degree of justification required for knowledge falls below certainty, we should look for a more informative characterization of "non-accidentally related,"[1] or else look for a different solution to the problem.

Another thing to notice is that the above three cases all *involve* a *false* justified belief. This might suggest amending the analysis in the following way. S knows that *P* at *t* if and only if:

1 *S* believes that *P* at *t*.

2 *P* is true.

3 *S* is justified in believing that *P* at *t*.

4 S does not base the belief that *P* on a false belief.

This analysis is a version of what is sometimes called the "no false lemmas" response to the Gettier problem. Since the three examples above all involve an inference based on a false belief, they fail condition (4), and do not count as knowledge according to this analysis. But is (4) really *necessary*? Aren't there cases of knowledge based on a false belief? Consider the following variant on the example from Russell:

Case 4: Smith believes that *the late Prime Minister's name is Balfour*, and believes this on the basis of good, justifying evidence. Smith also vividly recalls, correctly, that the late Prime Minister's initials are AJB. Smith infers that *the late Prime Minister's last name begins with a 'B'*.

In this case, despite the fact that Smith's belief is based *in part* on a false belief, it seems that Smith does know that the late Prime Minister's name begins with a 'B'. But perhaps we can allow such cases to count as cases of knowledge by the following modification. S knows that *P* at *t* if and only if:

1 *S* believes that *P* at *t*.

2 *P* is true.

3 *S* is justified in believing that *P* at *t*.

4 S's justification for believing that *P* at *t* does not depend *essentially* on a false belief.

Call this analysis the "no essential false lemmas" response to the Gettier problem. Since Smith would be justified in believing that the Prime Minister's name begins with 'B' even if he did not rely on his belief that the Prime Minister's name is Balfour, Smith's justification does not depend *essentially* on the latter false belief.

Are these conditions jointly sufficient for knowledge? Consider the following case:

Case 5: Smith is driving through the country and seems to see a red barn on a hill. He thereby comes to believe that *there is a red barn on that hill.* However, what he actually sees is just a barn façade. There is in fact a red barn on the hill, but it is on the other side of the hill, hidden by the façade.

One strategy for the defender of the false lemma view is to insist that Smith does depend essentially on a false belief, even if such a belief is not explicit. For Smith must have come to believe that there is a red barn on the hill by implicitly believing something to the effect that "*that* structure is a red barn." But now consider this famous sort of case:

Case 6: Smith is driving through the country and seems to see a red barn on a large hill. He thereby comes to believe that *that is a red barn.* Although his belief is true, the hill is covered in red barn façades, and he could have just as easily believed that one of these façades was a red barn.[2]

In this case, Smith's belief does not depend essentially on a falsehood, and many are inclined to deny that Smith knows that he sees a red barn. The proponent of the false lemma view might claim that a different false belief is involved in such cases: when forming ordinary beliefs about objects in one's environment there is something like a background belief to the effect that "there is nothing strange or peculiar about the environment in which I'm reaching this conclusion." If such a belief were in play, this might be the false belief that destroys knowledge. Such a "fix" is certainly controversial. More needs to be said about what might count as a "strange or peculiar" environment—surely not just any strange or peculiar feature of the environment would destroy knowledge—and some might worry that the account would counter-intuitively rule out knowledge in some cases just because the environment is abnormal or strange.

However, some are inclined to claim that this *is* a case of knowledge, and warn us not to take every sort of lucky accident to destroy the possibility of knowledge.

Does knowledge require epistemic certainty?

The literature on the Gettier problem is enormous, and there remains no consensus on how to solve it. Some might take this as a sign that we should give up one of the key assumptions needed to generate the problem. Recall that one of the assumptions was that knowledge does not require certain or infallible justification: one could know that *P* while having justification for the belief that *P* that does not entail or guarantee that truth of *P*. Suppose we take the Cartesian view instead and hold that knowledge requires a degree of justification that guarantees the truth. The combination of a JTB analysis with infallibilism seems to block the Gettier cases.

Of course, accepting infallibilism has some serious consequences. Very little of what we believe is infallibly justified, and so, if infallible justification is required for knowledge, very little of what we believe counts as knowledge. Unless we are happy with this result, we might hope for a different response to the Gettier problem, perhaps sticking with the modified analysis above, the one that adds the condition that there be no essential dependence on false beliefs. There are, however, other problems with the view that knowledge does not require certain or infallible justification. I will briefly mention three concerns here.[3]

The first challenge to the view that knowledge does not require epistemic certainty is that this seems to conflict with the plausible principle that if S knows that P and S knows that Q, and S competently deduces from this that P and Q, then S knows that P and Q. For suppose that S has some degree of justification that is barely sufficient for knowledge that P, and some degree of justification that is barely sufficient for knowledge that Q, whatever that degree of justification happens to be. Suppose also that these are each contingent and logically independent propositions. Assuming that we can, at least roughly, quantify degrees of justification using probabilities, that measure will presumably be somewhere between 0.5 and 1—say, 0.8. The probability of P and Q will be less than 0.8, since the probability of a conjunction of logically independent, contingent claims is less than the probability of either conjunct. But then, S wouldn't know P and Q after all, since S's justification for that conjunction would fall below the 0.8 threshold for knowledge.

The second, related concern has to do with the idea that there is some degree of justification, less than certainty, which (together with the other conditions for knowledge) is sufficient for knowledge. The worry is both simple and serious: it is difficult to see how any such assignment, whether for all contexts or within a particular sort of context, could fail to be arbitrary.

The third and final challenge I want to mention here concerns the oddness or infelicity of what are often called "concessive knowledge attributions," like "I know that P, but I could be wrong," or "I know that P, but it might be false that P." A very closely related concern is the fact that people tend to retract knowledge claims or retreat to a weaker claim when the possibility of error is made salient. Thus, when I ask you if you really know that your car is where you parked it given that cars get stolen all the time, you might be inclined to say that you know that it is *probable* that your car is there, but no longer assert that you do know. Infallibilists sometimes appeal to these infelicities and the inclination to retract or weaken knowledge claims when error possibilities are made salient to support the view that knowledge must rule out the possibility of error. There have been a number of fallibilist attempts to respond to such puzzles, many of which attempt to explain the oddness as having to do with norms of assertion, or a matter of what is and is not pragmatic to assert, rather than an incoherence in the very idea of fallible knowledge.[4]

Some central questions in epistemology

At a very general level, epistemologists have traditionally been concerned with two central issues: (1) What is it that we know or are at least justified in believing? That is, what is the *scope* or *extent* of our knowledge, and of our justified beliefs? (2) What is the *nature* and *structure* of knowledge or justification; how is knowledge or justification possible? We began this chapter with the latter question in discussing the traditional analysis of knowledge, and will continue to focus on it as we discuss the nature and structure of epistemically justified belief. But it will help to have a discussion of both questions and of their relation to the epistemologist's interest in skepticism.

We can distinguish varieties of skepticism on the basis of (a) the particular kind of *epistemic status* (e.g., knowledge, justification, rationality, certainty, etc.) the skeptic is denying or challenging, and (b) the *scope* or *range* of skepticism, i.e., the class of beliefs whose purported epistemic status is being denied or challenged. Perhaps a good case can be made that, traditionally, knowledge was the dominant status of interest, with skepticism regarding rationality or justification being of interest primarily as a component of knowledge. However, many contemporary epistemologists focus on rationality or epistemic justification, either because they take it to be a central requirement for knowledge, or because they take it to be interesting and important in its own right, independent of any contribution it might make to knowledge (or both). I will follow their lead here and focus on epistemically rational or epistemically justified belief.[5]

Global skepticism, the view that no belief whatsoever is justified, has the widest scope. It is *epistemically self-defeating* in the sense that its truth precludes one's being justified in accepting it: if global skepticism is true then one could never be justified in believing it.[6] A less global but still very radical form of skepticism denies that *any* of our *empirical* beliefs are justified. Traditionally, there have been few skeptics of either kind. A slightly less radical skepticism grants that we have justified empirical beliefs regarding the existence and character or content of our own present experiences, including the content of our apparent memories, but denies that we have any justified beliefs regarding our past experiences, our future experiences, or the world outside our minds. The latter class of empirical beliefs are often the primary targets of attack (for some unsurprising reasons that I will soon mention), but as the non-skeptic appeals to further empirical beliefs in response, the skeptic may attack either the inference from these empirical beliefs to belief in the external world, or attack the empirical premises believed, including beliefs about our past and future experiences. This skepticism is not strictly global, since the justification of some beliefs about our *present* experiences, apparent memories, and perhaps some other mental states may be granted.

We can also distinguish varieties of skepticism by the modality of their claims. Skeptics might argue that justification is logically, metaphysically, or physically impossible. Or they might grant, for sake of argument at least, that justification is possible in all these senses—in other words, that some physically possible sort of rational being would possess it—but still argue that justification is not available to us or to beings like us, perhaps because certain contingent facts beyond our control preclude *our* actually possessing it.

Why are traditional epistemologists so interested in skepticism, and why do they think engaging it is so central to epistemology? At a general level, the answer is that they are interested in explaining how justification is possible, and in ascertaining, in some philosophically or intellectually satisfying way, whether and which of our beliefs are in fact justified. Engaging with skepticism seems a practically, if not essentially, indispensable means to achieving these goals. The epistemologist's most central motivation for engaging skepticism is not some fear or paranoia that it might be true, or the need to refute actual skeptics, but the desire to better understand what justification involves, and how much of it we have. Our inability to address certain kinds of skepticism is likely to reflect important limitations on our rationality that it might be interesting and valuable to understand; "if skeptics did not exist, one might reasonably say, the serious epistemologist would have to invent them" (BonJour 1985: 15).

Let me say a little more about these two epistemological interests: understanding the nature of justification, and determining how much of it we have. First, the traditional epistemologist wants to understand justification *in general*, and not just some kind of justification on the basis of some other. In all kinds of ordinary and scientific contexts, we assume and even take for granted that we are justified in believing all sorts of things, and are content to take them as true in our deliberations, but when we are trying to understand what makes justification in general possible we ought to refrain from relying on such assumptions.

Second, we are not merely interested in understanding how justified belief might be possible in the abstract, for some rational being or other. Epistemologists are generally interested in developing and evaluating accounts that at least purport to apply to *us*, accounts which aim to show that we do have beliefs that are justified to some roughly specifiable degree, or show that, certain avoidable cognitive failings aside, nothing significant stands in the way of our acquiring justification for our beliefs. The logical, metaphysical, and even physical possibility of being justified are all compatible with its being extremely unlikely or practically impossible that we are actually justified in our beliefs. Perhaps conditions in the actual world preclude our ever having justified beliefs, or preclude having them except in very remote possibilities. For example, it might turn out that justification requires having access to good reasons or good evidence, but that we lack such access for most of what we believe. But so long as there remains a reasonable hope that justification is available to us, an epistemological account that aspires to explain how it is possible will be interesting.

True, traditional epistemologists are interested in a *philosophical account* of justification, and are likely to impose special constraints on what counts as a philosophically satisfactory position. They are interested, for example, in understanding justification *in general*, and not just justification for beliefs in some very specific domain; and they want to understand the very nature of justification itself, understand what is essential to it, and not just what causes or conditions are *normally* required for the acquisition of justification. But none of this entails that they are interested only in accounts pertaining to philosophers, or to agents with exceptional or superhuman cognitive abilities.

The epistemologist's interest in skepticism *regarding the external world* is motivated not only by the obvious fact that we hold beliefs about the external world, but by the apparently central cognitive and practical roles that beliefs about the world we inhabit play, the persistent intuition that some significant core of such beliefs are rational or justified, and the fact, reflected in the difficulty of responding to skeptical arguments, that it is far from obvious what gives these beliefs their positive epistemic status. Our external world beliefs, and the conviction that they are rational, are very much a part of common sense.

Of course, common sense says little more regarding the epistemic status of our ordinary beliefs about the external world than that they are *in some sense* rational or well-supported, and common usage of terms like "knowledge", "rational", etc., are not very precise. We cannot simply assume in our philosophizing that our commonsense notions are univocal, or that any non-skeptical solution must, at the end of the day, leave our commonsense beliefs unaffected. An epistemological theory that relies only on common-sense notions of *knowledge, rationality, belief,* and so on, providing no analysis or refinement of these notions, is unlikely to provide an illuminating epistemological account. Certain philosophical problems may ultimately force us to modify our initial concepts, or persuade us that we are not justified in quite the sense we were hitherto inclined to take ourselves to be. So long as we arrive at our modified views in motivated, principled, non-arbitrary ways, we may yet preserve an interesting and important sense of rationality or justi-fication that applies to us.

Foundationalism and the regress argument

If I am asked why I believe that I am mortal, I will probably answer that I believe all humans are mortal, and that I am human. If you ask me why I accept these beliefs, I will probably offer you still other claims I take to be true. For example, if you ask me why I think all humans are mortal, I will answer that there are no humans who have lived to be hundreds of years old, that all humans seem to age and their health deteriorate in ways that strongly suggest that the death of their bodies is inevitable, that alleged reports of immortality are rare and tend to come from biased or untrustworthy sources, and so on. Any justification I have for my belief that I am mortal thus seems to depend on the *inference* I draw from these other beliefs, or at least on the availability to me of such an inference—on my ability to provide or make such an inference.

Foundationalism about justification imposes certain structural constraints on a proper account of justified belief. Let us distinguish conceptually between *non-inferentially justified* beliefs, which are justified but do not depend for their justification on any inference from other beliefs, and *infer-entially justified* beliefs, which do depend on inference from other beliefs for their justification. Following common usage, I will also call the former *basic beliefs* or *foundationally justified beliefs*, and the latter *non-basic* or *non-foundational* justified beliefs. Foundationalism has come to be under-stood as any view according to which any justified belief must either be a basic belief, and so (given the above definition) be justified without depending on other beliefs for its justification, or else, if it is non-basic, depend for its justification ultimately and at least in part on basic beliefs. Notice that the above characterization of foundationalism entails that if any belief is justified, some beliefs must be basic.

Foundationalists have traditionally utilized some version of the epistemic regress argument in defense of their view. Here is a standard version of the argument:

1   Any justified belief must either be basic (non-inferentially justified) or non-basic (inferentially justified).

2   If a justified belief is non-basic, then it must be justified by an (actual or available) inference, and:

(a) the inference is infinitely regressive, with each belief in the inference requiring some further inference for its justification; or

(b) the inference is circular, so that the justified belief appears as a premise in its own justification; or

(c) the inference terminates with beliefs that are not themselves justified; or

(d) the inference terminates with beliefs that are basic.

3 An infinite regress cannot provide justification for a belief.

4 A circular inference cannot provide justification for a belief.

5 Unjustified beliefs cannot provide justification for other beliefs.

6 Therefore, any justified belief must either be basic, or depend for its justification on an inference that terminates with beliefs that are basic.

The first premise is unassailable. The rest of the argument proceeds by elimination, ruling out all but the last of the options mentioned in the second premise.

The first option (a) is to allow a belief to be justified by an inferential regress that extends infinitely. This is thought to be implausible for at least two reasons. First, it requires something no ordinary subject is capable of: possession of an infinite number of justifying beliefs, each of which is a belief with a different propositional content. Some might reply that this is not the case; it is only required that one *be able* to provide further reasons to support any belief that is challenged, and provide further reasons for those reasons, and so on as needed. But even if this is a plausible amendment, it will not help with the second problem: there seem to be obvious counterexamples, cases in which each belief is by hypothesis justified by other beliefs, but in which the resulting belief is surely not justified. Thus, for example, I might believe that there is at least one elf on my left shoulder, where my reason for this is the distinct belief that there are at least two elves on my shoulder, and believe that in turn because I believe that there are at least three elves on my shoulder, and so on ad infinitum.[7] Even assuming that it is possible for ordinary subjects to have, or have available to them, an infinite number of supporting beliefs or reasons of this sort, such a belief is intuitively not justified.

The second option (b) seems no better, for a circular inference seems obviously vicious: I cannot rely, even in part, on a belief in a proposition in order to justify a belief in the same proposition! (The coherentist might object at this point, claiming that not all circularity is bad, or, more plausibly perhaps, that the regress argument illegitimately assumes that justification must be linear in structure. We take up coherentism in the next chapter.)

What about (c)? It seems in principle possible to justify any belief of mine if all I need is some other unjustified belief that would, if true, constitute good evidence or good reasons for the proposition believed. The underlying concern is that there is no reason to think that beliefs justified in this way are true or likely since there is no reason to think that the "foundational" (unjustified!) beliefs that all other beliefs depend on for justification are true or likely. If I believe without justification that there are at least two elves on my left shoulder, then it seems on this view that I would be justified in believing that there is at least one elf on my left shoulder. That the latter belief is justified is implausible: why should anyone expect it to provide a reason or justification for the truth of the belief, given that the input belief is unjustified? The basic worry can be summarized by a slogan I have heard some philosophers use to dismiss this view: "garbage in, garbage out."

If each of these options are rejected then the only option left is the foundationalist one: that any inferentially justified belief must ultimately depend for its justification on beliefs that are basic or non-inferentially justified. It is worth noting that the argument does not establish that we have basic or foundationally justified beliefs; it establishes only that if any beliefs are justified then there must be some basic beliefs, and that any non-basic beliefs must ultimately depend for their justification on basic beliefs. If we add the premise that global skepticism about justification is false, that at least some beliefs are justified, then the argument allows us to conclude that there are some basic beliefs.

Internalist and externalist versions of foundationalism

We have at least a rough, initial idea of how non-basic beliefs could be justified: their justification depends on some inference that the subject actually makes—or at least, one that she is able to make, or that is in some significant sense available to her. What account can be given for the basic beliefs required to halt the inferential regress? Here's a start: in order for a belief to be basic or foundationally justified, the subject must have some good reason or evidence in favor of the truth of the proposition believed. Otherwise, even if the belief turns out to be true or highly likely, there is no clear reason that separates it from a dogmatic or unjustified belief that just happens to be true or probable. But what exactly does having such a reason or evidence involve?

Reflection on this question might suggest, against the foundationalist, that a regress is inevitable. Only something that can stand in an inferential or logical relation to a belief can provide a reason or evidence for the truth or probability of that belief, and only something that is itself a belief, or that is judgmental or belief-like, can stand in such a relation. So, only a belief, or something appropriately belief-like, can justify any allegedly basic belief. In order for it to provide such a reason or be able to justify a basic belief, this other belief or belief-like state must itself be justified. But then, the original allegedly basic belief turns out not to be basic after all.[8]

There are a number of ways the foundationalist might attempt to halt this regress. One is to reject the traditional requirement that the subject must have some good reason to think that the proposition believed is true in order for the belief to be justified. That is, one might reject the access-internalist requirement:

> **Awareness-internalism or access-internalism**: A subject S can be epistemically justified in believing that P only if S is aware of or has access to a reason in favor of the truth or probability of P.

An access- or awareness-externalist is someone who denies the above requirement for epistemic justification.

> **Awareness-externalism or access-externalism**: A subject S can be epistemically justified in believing that P without being aware of or having access to a reason in favor of the truth or probability of P.

Note that this is compatible with saying that some beliefs—inferential or non-basic beliefs, for example—require some sort of access to reasons. But access-externalists (henceforth simply "externalists") deny that access to reasons is always required; they may and often do deny that we have, let alone need, access to such reasons in the case of basic or foundationally justified beliefs. Externalist foundationalists do insist that a basic belief must satisfy some further condition(s) in order to be justified. For example, they might require that the belief be produced by a process that is "reliable"— roughly, a type of process that yields true beliefs more often than not.[9] The requirement that there be some objective connection to truth or probability is retained by many versions of externalism, but the requirement of access to reasons is dropped.

Many foundationalists would rather not give up access internalism. They refuse to give up the intuitive requirement that one have a reason to think that the belief has something going for it, something relevant to its truth or probability; the fact that it is true or probable in some objective sense, or that there are good reasons to take it to be true or probable, is not relevant to the subject's justification for the belief if the subject has no grasp of what the belief has going for it. Externalists themselves often admit that the access requirement is intuitive, though they argue that at the end of the day there are good reasons to give it up. We'll examine the internalist-externalist controversy in more detail later in the book, and as we'll see, the precise way to characterize the controversy is itself a matter of debate. We'll also see that there are stronger and weaker forms of internalism. But for now, let us consider some other ways that foundationalists have attempted to halt the regress and account for the justification of basic beliefs.

Mental state foundationalism vs. external world foundationalism

Rather than deny the access-internalist requirement, some foundation-alists have questioned the above argument's assumption that only a belief or something belief-like can provide a reason or evidence in favor of the truth of one's belief. I presently believe that I am thirsty, and my reason or evidence for this belief seems to be a certain experience I have, a feeling or experience of thirst. I also believe that I intend to get some water, and that I apparently remember placing my water bottle on the shelf behind me, and my reason or evidence in each case seems to be an experience of some sort—an experience of intending to do something, and an apparent memory, respectively. The underlying experiences might be belief-like in the sense of being propositional or having propositional content (see the discussion of intentionalism in the previous chapter), but they don't seem to be belief-like in the sense of involving any attitude of accepting, endorsing, or assenting to a proposition. Such things as believing, accepting, endorsing, or assenting to a proposition are the sort of acts that can be justified or unjustified, rational or irrational. The experiences just mentioned involve no such attitude; they are not the sorts of things that can be justified or unjustified, and so no further question of whether and how they might be justified is relevant.[10]

One interesting case, however, is that of beliefs *about one's own occurrent or conscious belief*. I know that I believe that I am mortal. What justifies my belief *that I believe that I am mortal*? Phenomenologically, what seems to happen is that upon considering the thought that I am mortal, I find myself aware of or conscious of my accepting, endorsing, or assenting to it. According to at least some traditional foundationalists, my meta-belief *that I believe that I am mortal* is justified because I have an awareness or consciousness of this attitude of accepting or endorsing the proposition *that I am mortal*.[11] We can distinguish between the awareness or consciousness of the attitude and the attitude itself. On a traditional view, this awareness or consciousness is not itself a belief or similar propositional attitude, though in this case (unlike the case of awareness of pain or thirst) the *object* of awareness, that *of which* one is aware, is a belief. Since this awareness of the attitude provides justi-fication for the meta-belief, and is not itself a belief or similar propositional attitude, it is not the sort of thing that can be justified or unjustified, and so no further question of whether and how it might be justified arises. The first-order belief *that I am mortal* may be true or not, justified or unjustified, but that does not affect the justification of my meta-belief *that I believe that I am mortal.* Traditional foundationalists can thus treat such introspective meta-beliefs as *basic,* for their justification does not depend on any (actual or available) *inference* from other beliefs.

Notice that the examples just given are all beliefs *about experiences or conscious mental states of some sort,* and the view being considered is that these beliefs are justified by our awareness of the experiences or conscious mental states they purport to describe or be about. Indeed, some founda-tionalists hold that the only beliefs that are basic are beliefs about our own experiences or mental states—or, more carefully, they hold that the only beliefs that are basic and whose justification is *a posteriori or empirical* rather than *a priori* are those beliefs that are about our own experiences or mental states. On most views, simple *a priori* beliefs, like the belief that 2+2=4, that triangles are trilateral, and that circles have no corners, may be basic but they are not *about* experiences or mental states.[12] Let us set these beliefs aside, which are concerned with necessary, *a priori* truths, and focus on contingent, *a posteriori* beliefs.

Mental state foundationalism (MSF): *S*'s belief is foundationally justified *a posteriori* only if it is a belief about one's own experiences or mental states.

A mental state foundationalist might accept internalism by claiming that beliefs about our mental states can be justified by a direct awareness of or direct introspective access to our own mental states. On such a view, it is because of this special or privileged access that we each have to at least some of our own mental states that we can directly justify certain beliefs about them. Take the belief that I am thirsty. I can be directly aware of my feeling of thirst in a way that others cannot; they must infer that I am thirsty from something else—from my testimony or behavior for example, or from some other source of information about me—while I need no such inference. If I am directly aware of feeling thirsty, then I have direct access to that which makes this belief true, and so seem to have access to as good a reason as I could ever want for the belief's truth. There are many other mental states that I can access directly. In addition to the examples already given, I am aware of different perceptual or sensory states. I am currently aware, for example, of various tactile, visual, and auditory experiences. I apparently feel the smooth keys of a laptop computer, apparently see a computer screen and two hands moving under the screen, apparently hear a cello playing in the background, and so on. The Cartesian reflections of the first chapter support the claim that we are directly aware *only* of these appearances—we can directly examine only our own mental states, experiences, or "ideas," and not the objects or events in the external world that these are appearances of.

I should say a bit more here regarding the sort of direct awareness that mental state foundationalists have traditionally appealed to in order to account for foundational justification and halt the regress of reasons. A direct awareness of X is an awareness of X that is not mediated by or does not depend on awareness of anything else. Many different views can accept that there is such a thing as direct awareness so understood. Traditional foundationalists add at least two related features to distinguish their sense of direct awareness or (as they sometimes call it, following Russell 1912) "acquaintance." First, direct awareness or acquaintance is a non-judgmental and non-conceptual form of awareness; it does not itself involve the forming of any judgment or thought, or the application of any concepts. Second, it is a real relation and so requires the existence of its relata (the things related); one cannot be directly aware of X or acquainted with X without X existing.[13] It is because traditional foundationalists doubt that we are ever acquainted with external world objects that they tend to deny that we can be foundationally justified in believing things about the external world.

The proponent of the anti-foundationalist argument of the previous section might find such appeals to direct awareness unsatisfactory. Whatever provides a reason or evidence in favor of the truth of the belief must stand in some sort of logical relation to the belief. It may be that one's having a particular sort of experience, or state of awareness, *causes* one to form a belief, but a mere causal relation is not a logical one. It seems that only something propositional can stand in such a relation, and so only something propositional can provide such a reason.[14] The foundationalist who insists that non-propositional states can provide such a reason can respond that there is a non-inferential but broadly logical, non-causal, relation at work here. The relevant relation between the belief and the mental state is a *descriptive* relation, or a relation of *correspondence*. Just as there must be an *inferential* relation of some sort between a justified belief and the inferred belief it justifies in order for the latter to be justified, there must be a relation of *correspondence* between the belief and the mental state it is about in order for the former to be justified. This applies just as much to beliefs about beliefs, as to beliefs about non-belief states.[15]

Many contemporary foundationalists reject MSF, and allow for empirical or
a posteriori beliefs that are not about mental states to count as basic. They
might do so either because they find it intuitive that some such beliefs—e.g.,
beliefs regarding external objects—are basic, or because they worry that MSF
leads to radical skepticism, a consequence they find unacceptable. Against
MSF, they hold the following:

External world foundationalism (EWF): Some beliefs regarding
contingent, external-world objects, events, or states of affairs can be
foundationally justified *a posteriori*.

Externalists about epistemic justification often take it to be an advantage of
their view that they can easily accept external world foundationalism. If, for
example, what is required for justification is that our beliefs in fact be reliably
produced or probable in some objective sense, and it is not required that
one have a good reason to think that they are reliable or probable, then there
seems no reason, in principle, why external world beliefs could not be foundationally justified. Our perceptual beliefs might be produced by a reliable
perceptual process that does not depend on any inference from other beliefs.

There are other ways to accept EWF, ways that might seem more in the
spirit of internalism rather than externalism. As we saw earlier, we might
be direct realists or naïve realists, holding that we can be directly aware of
external world objects or states of affairs, and not just of internal or mental
states, and take this direct awareness to be relevant to the justification of
belief that the relevant external world object exists, or that the relevant state
of affairs obtains. If direct awareness of something does not involve justified
belief about it, it provides justification without raising a further issue of justification in turn. Is this a version of access internalism? Yes, provided that direct
awareness of the external world objects, events, or states of affairs counts
as awareness of or access to a reason in favor of the truth of the relevant
external world belief (that an object exists, an event has transpired, or some
state of affairs obtains).

1   Construct a Gettier-style counterexample of your own against the traditional analysis of knowledge. Do any of the modified analyses suggested in the text avoid the counterexample? Can you amend the case in some way, or think of other examples of your own, that cause trouble for the modified analysis you are considering?

2   Suppose that you buy a lottery ticket. You hear that a billion tickets were sold, and there is one winner, though the winning number has not yet been announced. You know that it is *highly unlikely* that your ticket is the winner. However, do you know *that your ticket is not the winner*? Many tend to think that, intuitively, you do *not* know this. But aren't you at least justified in believing it? After all, the probability of winning is *extremely* low. What might explain the intuitive response? Do you know that your car or bike is where you left it? Do you know your birth date is correct? Do you know how many siblings you have? Are there ways in which these cases are different from the lottery case? What implications do these questions have for the relationship between knowledge and certainty?

3   According to access internalism, knowing or rationally believing something requires access to some reason or evidence in favor of its truth. However, people are not always very good at articulating these reasons. Can you think of some cases in which, intuitively, people know or at least have a rational or justified belief, but are particularly bad at offering such reasons? Is it possible that they nevertheless do have such access? We often claim of children, and even our pets and other animals, that they "know" certain things. Do they satisfy the access-internalist requirement?

For excellent general introductions to epistemology, see BonJour (2009), Audi (2010), Feldman (2003), and Fumerton (2006)—all of which have *Epistemology* as the main title.

For a collection of many influential attempts to solve the Gettier problem ("Is Justified True Belief Knowledge?" [1963]), see Pappas and Swain's *Essays on Knowledge and Justification* (1978). For a detailed examination of attempts to solve the Gettier problem of the early 1980s, see Shope (1983). Zagzebski (1994) criticizes the main attempted solutions and argues that none will work unless it holds that whatever is added to belief must *entail* truth.

For a survey of foundationalist theories, see Hasan and Fumerton's "Foundationalist Theories of Epistemic Justification" in the *Stanford Encyclopedia of Philosophy*. For recent defenses of classical foundationalism, which either require infallible or certain foundations, or are committed to the acquaintance theory or the doctrine of the given in some form, see BonJour (1999, 2003), Fales (1996), Fumerton (1995), and McGrew (1995). DePaul's *Resurrecting Old-Fashioned Foundationalism* (2001) includes essays on relatively traditional or classical forms of foundationalism, by BonJour and Fumerton, with some critiques by Pollock and Plantinga. For an influential, earlier critique of traditional and other forms of foundationalism see BonJour's "Can Empirical Knowledge Have a Foundation?" (1978) and *The Structure of Empirical Knowledge* (1985: Part I). BonJour's critique of traditional internalist foundationalism is inspired in part by Sellars' famous attack on "the given" in "Empiricism and the Philosophy of Mind" (1956: Part I).

For more moderate, contemporary forms of foundationalism, see Chisholm's *The Foundations of Knowing* (1982) and *Theory of Knowledge* (1989), Audi's *The Structure of Justification* (1993), and Huemer's *Skepticism and the Veil of Perception* (2001: Ch. 5).

For readings on coherentism, and the internalist/externalist debate, see the suggestions at the end of the sixth and eighth chapters, respectively.

5

Coherentism

This chapter introduces the reader to the coherentist theory of epistemic justification. We begin by motivating the theory, examining its reply to the foundationalist regress argument and its objection to the foundationalist alternative. We then turn to the difficult question of how to understand the concept of coherence. Much of the chapter is then focused on central problems with coherentism that stem from the fact that, for the coherentist, the epistemic justification of beliefs doesn't depend on any observational or experiential input from the world, problems that seem to show that, for the coherentist, epistemic justification is not connected to the truth. We discuss the influential suggestion that we can accommodate something like observation into the system with the idea of cognitively spontaneous beliefs (beliefs that may be caused by perceptions but not justified by them). However, in the course of examining that suggestion a more serious problem emerges: the problem that coherentism seems unable to accommodate access to one's own beliefs.

The regress problem and conceptions of coherence

The coherentist rejects the view that justification requires a foundation of beliefs that do not depend on any other beliefs for their justification. On the coherentist view, beliefs are justified by virtue of their *coherence* with other beliefs. Epistemologists often compare the two by use of metaphors: the foundationalist insists that the structure of one's justified beliefs involves a *foundation* of beliefs that holds the rest of the structure up; the coherentist, on the other hand, claims that the justification that any belief has depends on the fact that it is part of a *web* of beliefs; the stability, we might say, of any particular part of the web depends on the structure of the whole. Coherentists have sometimes also used the metaphor of a raft at sea, one that can be rebuilt or repaired piece by piece on the open sea, with no particular plank or piece of the raft being indispensable. But these metaphors are likely to be misleading and we need to understand exactly what it is that the epistemologist—and in this chapter, the coherentist—is proposing.

We can begin to get a better idea of coherentism by examining the coherentist response to the regress argument for foundationalism. The coherentist might initially be understood as embracing the view that the regress of justification proceeds in a circle, with the very same belief ultimately appearing as a premise in its own justification. The problem is that embracing circular reasoning or circular inferences seems vicious. Suppose you ask me why I believe that an all-good God exists, and I tell you that I have had a religious experience that revealed God's existence and goodness to me. Suppose you then ask me why I believe I can trust this experience, and I answer that an all-good God exists and such a God would not allow me to be deceived by such an experience. You would not, and should not, be satisfied with this justification. Even granting for sake of argument that an all-good God would not allow me to be deceived, it is obviously illegitimate to defend my belief in God by appealing to the very belief that is in question. Nor does the problem go away by making the circle larger, employing a more elaborate inference that ultimately relies on the same belief. I cannot rely, even in part, on a belief in a proposition in order to justify a belief in the same proposition!

The coherentist might reply by granting that circular inferences are *dialectically* ineffective, that it is illegitimate to provide a circular argument in defending a claim to another person. But is the coherentist suggesting that, nevertheless, a circular inferential justification is not vicious, despite being dialectically useless or problematic? Coherentists often reply by rejecting the linear, one-directional structure foundationalists assume justification to have, and accepting a holistic view of justification instead; the coherentist replaces the idea of linear dependence between beliefs with that of mutual or reciprocal support. A particular belief might, in a particular context, be justified by inference from other beliefs. But according to coherentism any particular belief depends for its justification on the fact that it belongs to a *coherent set or web* of beliefs. It is the entire *set or web* of beliefs (or perhaps some significant sub-set of beliefs) that is justified in the primary sense, in virtue of its coherence, and particular beliefs are justified in virtue of belonging to or being members of that coherent set. To put essentially the same point in a different way, any particular belief depends for its justification on its coherence with the rest of one's beliefs.[1]

What exactly is *coherence*, and how do individual members of a belief set contribute to its coherence? Understanding coherence as consistency with the rest of one's beliefs is obviously too weak (and, as we'll soon see, arguably too strong as well). It is too weak, for a set of beliefs may be logically consistent simply because the beliefs are about utterly unrelated things. They don't conflict, but that's just because they aren't really talking about the same things. A set of beliefs that is not only logically consistent but some members of which support other beliefs is intuitively more coherent than one with the same number of beliefs that exhibits mere logical consistency. Moreover, we want to be able to make sense of coherence as something that is a matter of degree; understanding coherence purely in terms of consistency does not allow us to do so.

An early proposal is to understand coherence in terms of consistency and logical relations between beliefs: a set of beliefs is coherent just in case the set is consistent, and every belief in the set follows logically from the other beliefs in the set.[2] And perhaps we can take the degree of coherence to be determined, somehow, by the number of logical relations between beliefs in the system.

However, there are two serious problems with such a proposal. First, it seems *too strong* a requirement for coherence. Take, for example, the following three propositions: A school bus is approaching the corner and slowing down; some school kids are waiting on the corner; the school bus is about to stop at the corner. Intuitively, these propositions are coherent, but none of the propositions follows logically from the others: any two of these propositions are consistent with the denial of the third. Second, as Fumerton (1995) argues, coherence is also *too easy* to come by. He gives the example of adding to one's system of beliefs other beliefs that are trivially entailed by some of the propositions one already believes, and that trivially entail some of the propositions one already believes. A set of beliefs can thus have its coherence greatly enhanced in this way, but it seems absurd to say that this would indeed increase the justification of these beliefs.

The natural proposal at this stage is to understand coherence not simply in terms of consistency and entailment, but also *merely probabilistic* relations between beliefs: a set of beliefs can be more coherent if each belief is made more probable by the other beliefs in the set.[3] This would handle the first problem just raised. However, if logical or entailment relations still count towards coherence, it seems that the second problem remains.

Perhaps in part due to some of these problems, more recent accounts of coherence are more complex and sophisticated. Some coherentists who want to allow that non-deductive relations between beliefs contribute to coherence prefer to characterize coherence in terms of the presence of inferential connections between beliefs rather than, or in addition to, characterizing it in terms of probabilistic connections. Some have claimed that the coherence of a system of beliefs is enhanced by inductive and explanatory inferential connections between its component beliefs (e.g., BonJour 1985). As one adds more related beliefs to a system, the number of inferential connections goes up, and so does the coherence. This raises a problem that is similar to the problem Fumerton raised above: can't one keep raising the coherence of a belief simply by adding more inferentially related beliefs? Intuitively, we don't want to encourage adding more beliefs just for the sake of adding to the number of inferential connections between them; the set of beliefs would say more and more about the world, and it seems that we would be taking more of a risk of error, and have less probable beliefs as a result. (We'll return to this issue shortly, when we discuss problems with coherentism.) A more plausible view would be to measure coherence by something like "inferential density" rather than the mere number of inferences—that is, take the coherence to increase with increase in the number of (non-trivial?) inferential connections *per belief*. The more complex analyses of coherence in terms of various forms of inference raise difficult questions about how to measure the contribution that these various inferences or connections make to coherence and to the probability of one's beliefs. But let's suppose for sake of argument that these questions can be answered.[4]

We've seen that coherentists would (and should) deny that mere consistency is sufficient for justification-conferring coherence. Logical consistency of one's entire belief set is also arguably *not necessary* for justification. I believe a great many things, and it is possible, indeed likely, that I have some mutually inconsistent beliefs. In fact, I sometimes discover that I have or have had inconsistent beliefs, and just didn't notice the inconsistency. I might believe that it is Thursday, and believe that Thursday is garbage day, and yet believe that it is not garbage day today. Of course, once I become conscious of this inconsistency, I correct it in some way: I revise my belief that it is not garbage day (and then proceed to take the garbage out, hoping I am not too late). But the inconsistency was already there. Surely, though, the presence of this inconsistency in my belief set does not imply that all my beliefs are unjustified—or even that my belief that it is Thursday or that Thursday is garbage day is unjustified!

The problem is in fact more serious, for while at least one of the beliefs in the above example might, intuitively, be unjustified, it seems that we could be justified in holding every belief in a set of internally inconsistent beliefs, and do so even when we know that the beliefs are inconsistent! Richard Foley (1979) defends this and raises it as a serious problem for coherentism. Suppose we know that a very large number—say, a billion—lottery tickets are sold, and that only one of these is the winning ticket, though we don't yet know which it is. If I have one of these lottery tickets, the chance of it being a winner is so low that I seem justified in believing that it is a loser. But this is true of every ticket taken on its own: I am justified in believing, of it, that it is a losing ticket. These justified beliefs, taken together, conflict with my belief that one of these tickets is the winning ticket; these beliefs are mutually inconsistent, and I know it. But it does not seem that this inconsistency affects my justification for any belief in this set. Or, to give another example, I might justifiably believe, of every sentence in a particular book, that it is true, while also believing that the book is bound to contain some errors or falsehoods, at least one sentence that is false. Something similar applies to our perspective on our own beliefs: I might have justification for accepting the truth of every belief in a set, but also, recognizing my fallibility, be justified in believing that at least some of these beliefs are false, and so be justified in holding inconsistent beliefs, since it cannot be that all the propositions I believe are true and that at least one of them is false.[5] It seems best, therefore, to drop the requirement that one's beliefs be mutually or internally consistent in order for any member belief to be justified, but to do so is, as Foley puts it, to give up the very heart of coherentism (1979: 257). BonJour (1989) agrees with Foley that logically inconsistent beliefs can be justified, but denies that consistency is essential to coherentism, claiming that coherentist accounts can be developed without it. Some contemporary epistemologists sympathetic to coherentism still take this to be a serious problem, though they have not given up hope of solving it.[6]

We can now distinguish between strong foundationalism and a hybrid view that we can call weak foundationalism (sometimes also called foundherentism). According to strong foundationalism, foundational beliefs have a degree of justification that does not derive from inference or coherence, a degree sufficient to satisfy the justification condition for knowledge or to justify other beliefs. According to weak foundationalism, foundational beliefs require only a degree of justification that is too low to satisfy the justification condition on knowledge or too low to justify other beliefs; coherence can add to the justification and yield beliefs that do satisfy the justification condition on knowledge and can justify other beliefs. All forms of foundationalism hold that for any belief to be justified there must be some that have a degree of justification without depending on other beliefs for that justification, but weak foundationalism allows that the degree of justification for foundational beliefs is lower than required for it to justify other beliefs and can be raised by its coherence with other beliefs. We will focus on pure (or "strong") foundationalism and pure coherentism.

The isolation objection, the alternative systems objection, and observational beliefs

Let us suppose that the problems with finding an adequate and defensible conception of coherence can be solved, and consider other problems that are more directly related to perceptual justification. One very natural, indeed obvious, objection to coherentism is often called the *isolation objection*. If all that matters for justification is that one's system of beliefs be coherent, where coherence has only to do with the beliefs themselves and the relations between them, why should that provide any reason or assurance that these beliefs are true, or that they correspond in any way to reality? One's system of belief might thus be "isolated" from reality and yet remain entirely coherent. Another natural and closely related objection is the *alternative systems objection*. For any given set or system of beliefs, there are indefinitely many equally coherent but incompatible, alternative systems of belief. If these are all equally coherent, then coherentism provides no way to decide between them, no way to determining which of these is true or at least likely to be true. The underlying worry of both objections is that epistemically justified beliefs must be probable, truth-conducive, or indicative of truth in some way, but coherence alone fails to satisfy this requirement.[7]

Unlike coherentism, various forms of foundationalism can allow experiences to play a role in the justification of beliefs. These experiences serve to "anchor" our beliefs to reality, or keep them from being totally isolated from reality; and they provide a crucial constraint on the contents of our beliefs. Thus, while the general truth-conducivity of a system of beliefs is by no means an immediate or trivial result for the foundationalist, the epistemic role assigned to experience or observation seems to block the isolation objection and the alternative systems objection. Indeed, it seems that the problem with coherentism is precisely that it fails to assign an epistemic role to experience or observation.

This might suggest a way that coherentism can respond to the isolation and alternative systems objections. Indeed, a prominent response to these objections is to allow experiential, perceptual, or observational *beliefs* to play a special role without serving as foundational or non-inferentially justified beliefs. This might seem paradoxical: experiential, perceptual, or observational beliefs by definition depend on some non-belief state—an experience or perception of some sort. But then, their justification cannot depend on any inference, and so must be non-inferential in nature. In response, coherentists might allow that some empirical beliefs be non-inferentially *produced* or have a non-inferential *origin* or *source*, so that they are not the result of any *actual inference*, while denying that these or any other beliefs are non-inferentially *justified*. These perceptual beliefs depend *causally* (at least in part) on our sensory or perceptual experiences; they do not depend on experiences for *justification*, and the spontaneous character of these perceptual beliefs makes them suitable to play a broadly "observational" role as compared to non-spontaneous, inferred beliefs.

But how, exactly, could such beliefs be justified and contribute to the justification of other beliefs? Reflecting on this question exposes a serious problem for coherentism. To see the problem, let's consider one particular response to the question provided by BonJour (1985: Ch. 6). According to BonJour, we can accept a relatively broad understanding of "observation" as involving a process or mechanism that produces *spontaneous beliefs* about some range of subject matter. One's justification for a particular spontaneous belief would take the following form:

1 I have a spontaneous belief B, formed in circumstances of sort C.

2 Spontaneous beliefs formed in circumstances of sort C are highly reliable.

So (probably)

3 B is highly reliable, and so (probably) true.

This inference—or rather, the specific inference of which this is a mere form or schema—need not be explicit. The inference must be available to the subject, in some rough or implicit way. What makes a particular perceptual or other spontaneous belief justified is the fact that the subject has available to him or her some inference of this sort, and has that available "internally" as it were, without depending on the acquisition of any further evidence or information. The spontaneous beliefs are thus justified by their being inferable from other beliefs, despite being non-inferentially produced. Moreover, notice that the inference supporting the observational or spontaneous belief B itself depends on observation, and in a couple of ways: knowledge or justified belief that the conditions of observation C obtain itself depends on present observation, and knowledge that these conditions are reliable is an empirical matter that will depend on perceptual beliefs, or on memorial beliefs or beliefs about the past that are themselves spontaneous. These further "observations" or spontaneous beliefs will themselves be justified by the availability of inferences of the same sort, and so we see already the sense in which coherence or mutual support is central to justification on this model.

A consequence of this coherentist or holist view is that the justification for perceptual beliefs and beliefs about the reliability of perception cannot be acquired *piecemeal*. The subject might acquire various beliefs and dispositions to form beliefs, including dispositions to form perceptual beliefs, before having justification for them. Once there is enough coherence between such perceptual beliefs about particular goings on, and about the conditions in which they are formed, and about the reliability of such beliefs, the subject acquires justification for having them, with the degree of justification increasing with the degree of coherence, in line with something like the criteria of coherence already discussed above.

The problem of internal access

There is, however, a problem that arises when we ask about the subject's justification for the very first premise of the inference—more specifically, the first part of the premise: I have a spontaneous belief B. Not only is the particular belief B a spontaneous belief, but the premise *that I have a spontaneous belief B* is or expresses a spontaneous belief, though an introspective rather than perceptual one: it is a belief about an internal mental state rather than something external. Let's call this belief B*. What is it that justifies B*? If it, too, is a spontaneous belief, it will presumably be justified by an inference of the same form:

1   I have a spontaneous introspective belief B*, formed in circumstances of sort C*.

2   Spontaneous introspective beliefs formed in circumstances of sort C* are highly reliable.

So (probably)

3   B is highly reliable, and so (probably) true.

Now, perhaps when it comes to introspective beliefs we can drop the part about B* being formed under certain conditions C*. Perhaps, intuitively, introspective beliefs are reliable or likely in such a wide range of cases that we don't need that qualification. Let's assume this is right. But let's focus on the first premise. How am I justified in believing *that I have a spontaneous introspective belief B*? Call this belief B**. Well, since this too is presumably a spontaneous belief, I would have to have yet another inference of the same sort available to me, with a first premise to the effect *that I have an introspective spontaneous belief B***, and a second premise to the effect that such beliefs are highly reliable or highly likely to be true. Perhaps I will not need to actually have such higher-level beliefs, but at the very least such inferences will have to be available and the higher-level beliefs must be ones I could form as needed.

If the justification of perceptual and other spontaneous beliefs takes this form, we seem to have given up the purely coherentist view for a form of infinitism. But, however we label such a view, it seems to be afflicted with a problem similar to the one we considered in discussing the infinitist response to the regress problem in the previous chapter. It is implausible that we have or even could form such higher-level beliefs beyond the first few iterations. Suppose I have the belief *that I see an apple*. My spontaneous introspective belief would be *that I believe that I see an apple*. The next level spontaneous introspective belief would be *that I believe that I believe that I see an apple*, and the next, *that I believe that I believe that I believe that I see an apple*, and so on. It seems highly implausible that I actually be able to form such higher-level beliefs once I get to the fifth or sixth levels, let alone be able to form infinitely many such introspective beliefs!

Perhaps there is a way out of this problem for coherentists. We have, after all, been considering one specific response to the problem of sensory or perceptual input for coherentism, and perhaps other responses are not vulnerable to this worry. If all that is required for justification is that one's beliefs satisfy conditions of coherence to some degree, then perhaps spontaneous beliefs can satisfy conditions of coherence, even if not quite in the way that BonJour suggests, at least not in every instance or at every level, and we can thereby avoid the hierarchical regress. Why isn't it sufficient that we have beliefs about the reliability of various spontaneous beliefs, that we have particular spontaneous beliefs, and perhaps other beliefs, where all these beliefs cohere with each other?

The problem is that so long as the coherentist accepts the access-internalist requirement, as traditional coherentists have, the problem cannot be avoided. According to access internalism, in order for a belief to be justified, the subject must have cognitive or internal access to good reasons in favor of that belief. So, given that on the coherentist view one's reasons for any particular belief will consist in the entire coherent set of beliefs, one will need to have some form of access to one's set of beliefs. But any such access must take the form of some other meta-belief to the effect that one believes such-and-such. But, by hypothesis, the subject had no such meta-belief. Even if we imagine adding this meta-belief to one's belief set, this solves nothing: the subject will need to have access to this meta-belief as well, and so the subject will require some further meta-belief. But, by hypothesis, the subject did not have this belief, and so is unable to satisfy the requirement of access to the beliefs in one's allegedly coherent beliefs set, and so no belief is justified!

It might seem that this is too quick. Perhaps all that is required for a belief to be justified is access to reasons in support of or reasons that cohere with it, not access to all of one's beliefs. Can the coherentist avoid the problem raised above in this way? No. Take any belief B. In order for that belief to be justified, the subject must have access to reasons—i.e., other beliefs—that support or cohere with B. Call such beliefs collectively R(B). So, the subject must have access to R(B) in order for B to be justified. But any such access to reasons R(B) will have to take the form of a meta-belief (or perhaps a set of meta-beliefs) to the effect that one believes R(B)—a belief that is not already included in R(B). Call such a belief B(R(B)). This meta-belief will itself have to be justified if it is to constitute a form of access that is epistemically relevant. But then, in order for it to be justified, the subject must have access to reasons that support or cohere with it—call such reasons R(B(R(B))). The form of access requires having some further belief, B(R(B(R(B)))). And so on. We thus see that the problem does generalize, provided that one accepts the access-internalist requirement.

One way out of this second problem is to drop the internal-access requirement. However, once one gives up this requirement and embraces externalism about epistemic justification, the motivation for resisting foundationalism becomes less clear.

Summary

Coherentism has been motivated in part by the perceived failure of internalist foundationalism to make sense of non-inferentially justified belief, and the need for an internalist alternative to foundationalism. One of the challenges for the coherentist is to offer a positive conception of coherence, one that allows us to compare alternative systems of belief and determine the degree of justification of particular beliefs within these systems. While some progress has been made on this front, we lack anything close to a complete and problem-free account of coherence. But even granting that these details can be satisfactorily filled in, a central problem that emerges for coherentism is that, ironically, it cannot satisfy the internalist requirement that is its central motivation. One might avoid the difficulty by dropping the internalist requirement entirely. After all, coherentism itself is a thesis about the structure of justification, and is not as such committed to access internalism. However, once one gives up this requirement and embraces externalism about epistemic justification, the motivation for resisting foundationalism becomes less clear.[8] Alternatively, one might hold onto internalism, and reconsider the possibility of internalist foundationalism.

1 Think of a specific, controversial belief of yours. It might be a belief falling in a domain of science, politics, religion, morality, or something else. You may know others who have very different beliefs in one of these particular areas. You may each defend your particular beliefs by appeal to other beliefs, such that each of you have relatively coherent systems or sub-systems of belief in that domain. How would you try to convince them to change their views? If you seem unable to appeal to beliefs they already have, what could you do to change their beliefs? If you adopt the coherentist view, are you committed to holding that they may be just as rational as you are in your views?

2 Consider a particular sensory experience of yours—say, one involving a distinctive, if not entirely familiar, smell or taste. Perhaps it is a smell or taste you cannot quite identify readily, but is certainly vivid and distinctive. How would you describe the experience to someone else? How would a coherentist attempt to explain your justification for believing that your description is correct?

3 Consider a belief of yours with a specific content, one that you are quite confident you hold. Suppose someone asks you how it is you know or have justification for believing that you hold this particular belief. What would you say? Is your answer compatible with coherentism?

Murphy's "Coherentism in Epistemology," in the *Internet Encyclopedia of Philosophy*, is a good introduction to the general topic. For more formal examinations of coherentism and its relation to probability, see Olson's entry on "Coherentist Theories of Epistemic Justification" (2012) in the *Stanford Encyclopedia of Philosophy*.

Important proponents of coherentism in the history of philosophy include some British idealists (e.g., Bradley and Bosanquet), and some philosophers of science (e.g., Neurath, Hempel, Quine, and especially Sellars). BonJour's *Structure of Empirical Knowledge* (1985) and Lehrer's *The Theory of Knowledge* (1990) provide clearer accounts, and much needed development. Bender's *The Current State of the Coherence Theory* (1989) is a collection of essays on the coherentism of BonJour and Lehrer, with their replies. Excellent critical discussions are also provided by Fumerton in *Metaepistemology and Skepticism* (1995: Ch. 5), and by BonJour after his conversion to foundationalism, in *Epistemic Justification* (2003: Ch. 3). More recent defenses of coherentism include Lycan's "Explanationist Rebuttals" (2012) and Poston's *Reason and Explanation* (2014).

6

Abductivism

In this chapter we consider a contemporary version of the broadly Lockean, "abductivist" reply to skepticism about the external world, according to which we are justified in believing in the external world because it provides the best explanation of experiential regularities. We introduce the idea of inference to the best explanation, and motivate two central explanatory criteria to guide our comparison of hypotheses or explanations, explanatory power and simplicity. We then show that the real world hypothesis (RWH), which corresponds very roughly to common sense, provides a very good explanation of regularities in experience. We then discuss four main challenges to abductivism: two that challenge the principle of inference to the best explanation itself (that the best might only be the "best of a bad lot," and that its being more likely than each skeptical alternative doesn't make it more likely than the disjunction of alternatives), one that challenges the claim that it is better than the skeptical scenarios, and one that challenges the claim that we have a broad and robust enough foundation of basic beliefs as ground for abduction. Some promising, though tentative, responses are offered to each of these objections. We end by considering the possibility of combining a version of abductivism with external world foundationalism (EWF).

Back to foundationalism

In the previous chapter we saw that internalist forms of coherentism face significant and arguably decisive problems, while externalist forms of coherentism seem unmotivated. We therefore return here and in the rest of the book to epistemological theories that are broadly foundationalist in structure. We can begin by recalling the distinction between two kinds of foundationalism regarding empirical belief. According to *mental state foundationalism* (MSF), of all empirical beliefs only beliefs regarding one's own mental states, appearances, sense data, or their properties can be foundationally justified or basic. According to *external world foundationalism*

(EWF), at least some beliefs about the external world can be foundationally justified or basic. Historically, a great many philosophers accepted MSF, but today an increasing number of foundationalists accept some form of EWF. In the remaining chapters we discuss the most prominent versions of the latter: phenomenal conservatism or dogmatism, externalism, and disjunctivism.

In the present chapter we discuss the possibility of justifying external world beliefs inferentially. More specifically, we consider the most prominent version of such a reply to skepticism, sometimes called "abductivism," according to which external world beliefs are justified by a kind of explanatory or "abductive" inference from beliefs about our own experience. This fits naturally with the traditional view that accepts MSF but denies EWF. However, it is worth noting that abductivism is compatible with views that reject MSF. Some coherentists, including BonJour (1985: 183–5), before his conversion to foundationalism, have offered abductivist responses to skepticism. Even some proponents of EWF have offered abductivist replies to skepticism, claiming that while beliefs about the external world can be justified foundationally, they can also be justified inferentially, with the result that the "unsoundness of skepticism is overdetermined" (Huemer 2015: 1033, fn. 4). Our focus here will be on the case for an inferential, abductivist justification of external world beliefs. We will, however, end by considering the possibility of a kind of abductivism according to which external world beliefs are justified because they best explain our experiences or appearances, but where no beliefs about our experiences or appearances are required. That would be a view that combines EWF and abductivism, and does not merely consider them to be two separate ways to justify external world beliefs.

Recall a central lesson from our reflections on Descartes and Hume: our knowledge of our own experiences or appearances is on relatively firm ground, but there is no deductive route from the nature of experiences to the character of the external world, and simple induction (i.e., "enumerative" induction that involves generalizing from observed correlations) can't help, since there is no way to peer behind the veil of perception and check that our experiences actually correspond to reality, and so no way to establish a correlation between our ideas or appearances and the real world as a ground for an inductive generalization. A natural strategy to pursue that is compatible with MSF is the abductive or explanationist one suggested, at least implicitly, by Locke, and recently defended by BonJour (1999) and Vogel (1990, 2008a): the existence of an external world of spatial objects provides a powerful explanation of various regularities experienced, a better explanation than the skeptical alternatives.

Inference to the best explanation (IBE)

Abduction or inference to the best explanation (IBE) is a widely used and arguably indispensable form of inference. IBE is used frequently in scientific reasoning: a specific hypothesis might be justified on the grounds that its truth *explains* the data collected or observations made, and *does so better than* the competing hypotheses. But IBE seems just as indispensable in ordinary, practical reasoning: my belief that a burglar broke into my house, for example, might be justified on the grounds that it *explains* my observations (a window is broken, and a number of valuables are missing), and *does so better than* any competing hypotheses.

Scientists tend to take for granted that there exists a spatial world and that they are able to causally interact with other things, including papers, computers, measuring instruments, collaborators, experimental subjects, and so on. In practical contexts we tend to make the same or very similar assumptions. I assume, for example, that windows and burglars exist, that I own certain objects, that these objects tend not to spontaneously disappear, and so on. We ordinarily take it as obvious that we acquire knowledge of our world on the basis of sensory experience or sensory perception, and that such knowledge plays a central cognitive and practical role in our lives. Upon reflection, however, it is far from obvious how exactly our apparent perceptions do or even could contribute to our knowledge. Indeed, as we have seen, skeptical arguments have led some to question whether we have any knowledge or even rational or justified belief regarding the world outside our minds.

The abductivist attempts to utilize IBE to justify belief in the external world. According to the abductivist, the best explanation of the fact that I have such-and-such familiar patterns of experience is that I exist in a world of relatively determinate spatial objects of various sorts, including my own body. What makes my belief in the existence of a physical or spatial world of this sort justified is that the truth of the belief is the best explanation of my having the sorts of experiences I do have.

What exactly is involved in an IBE inference? What is it that makes one explanation better than another? Various explanatory criteria have been offered, but in the context of abductivism or the debate over external world skepticism, something like the following criteria are often prominent:

Explanatory power. Other things being equal, a hypothesis is better the more experiential data it explains.

Simplicity. Other things being equal, simpler explanations are preferable to more complex ones. This applies to both types and tokens.[1]

- Other things being equal, the fewer the *types* or *kinds* of contingent entities, processes, causal, or lawful regularities (etc.) posited, the better.

- Other things being equal, the fewer the *token* contingent entities, processes, causal, or lawful regularities (etc.) posited, the better.

It is important to pay attention to both explanatory power and simplicity. We can increase the explanatory power of a hypothesis by positing more explainers, and we can keep simplifying a hypothesis by explaining less and less. What we really want is a combination of simplicity and explanatory power; we want to explain more with less. This naturally leads us to look for an explanation of the data that is "unified" in the sense that it involves a relatively small set of interconnected explainers that together account for a great deal of data, as opposed to a hypothesis with *piecemeal* explanations, i.e., one that posits various unconnected explainers, each of which explains only some specific observation or relatively narrow range of data.

Explanatory power and simplicity are commonly regarded to be explanatory virtues. But are they *epistemically relevant* virtues? Are they relevant to the aim of truth? A serious examination of these questions would lead us too far into technical territory, but it will help to have some motivation for thinking that they are indeed relevant to truth or probability.[2]

First, consider explanatory power. Suppose I have some surprising bit of evidence—say, for example, that my car won't start. Now, there are a handful of hypotheses which, if true, would explain or make it highly probable that my car won't start: for example, that my car battery is dead, that my starter is malfunctioning, or that I am doing something wrong (e.g., that it is a manual transmission and I am not depressing the clutch, or that it is an automatic and I have it in "drive"). Given that the car battery's being dead would raise the probability that my car won't start, the fact that I find that the car won't start raises the probability that car battery is dead, and lowers the probability that the car battery is fine. That is presumably why I begin to worry that perhaps my car battery is dead upon finding out that the car won't start. More generally, if the truth of a hypothesis H raises the probability of some evidence E, then, other things being equal, observing E raises the probability of H. And, other things being equal, the more H raises the probability of E, the more the observation of E raises the probability that H.

It would help to motivate the epistemic relevance of explanatory power in a way that does not depend on background empirical knowledge in the way that the above example does. Consider the fact that you presently seem to be reading, or have an experience as of words on a page. There are indefinitely many ways your experiences could have been, but they presently take on a very specific form. Now compare two hypotheses: On the one hand, there is the hypothesis that someone has authored these words and attempted to make them available to you, to transmit them to you, by some causal process or combination of processes (whether via sense organs you have, or some other way). On the other hand, there is the hypothesis that you are dreaming. Both hypotheses are *compatible* with the experience you are having, that of reading words on a page. The first hypothesis, however, makes it more likely that you are having the specific experience of reading as compared to the dream hypothesis; it explains the data better; it makes it much less surprising that you experience what you do. That is why your experience provides better evidence for the first hypothesis than the second. The hypothesis that you are dreaming may make it unsurprising that you experience what you do, but given that you could have dreamed all sorts of other things, it doesn't make it that much more likely that you are experiencing what you do.

Now, we could consider a more specific version of the dream hypothesis: you are dreaming *that you are holding a book in your hand*. That would make it more likely that you experience what you do. But when we do this, we increase what I am calling the explanatory power of a hypothesis only by also increasing the complexity of the hypothesis. And that may have some bearing on the probability of the hypothesis as well. Let us turn, then, to consider why simplicity is an explanatory virtue.

While explanatory power can thus raise the probability of a hypothesis given certain evidence, other factors can lower its probability. In particular, the *complexity* of a hypothesis can lower its probability. Why so? Again, a serious examination of this issue will take us far into technical territory; here I will only provide some intuitive motivation for this claim. Frist, suppose that you believe that H, and I believe that H&H* (where H and H* are each contingent propositions, and neither is logically entailed by the other). Suppose we also have exactly the same evidence, and that H and H&H* have the same explanatory power—to keep things simple, suppose they each entail the evidence at hand. We should favor H over H&H*, for there seems to be a clear sense that in accepting H&H* I am taking a greater risk of believing falsely than you are, and so the probability of H&H* is, all else equal, lower than the probability of H alone. For example, given that my car won't start, the probability that the battery is dead is lower than the probability that the battery is dead *and* the starter is broken; and the probability that the starter is broken is lower than the probability that the starter is broken *and* the battery is dead.

This is the easy case. What do we do when we want to compare hypotheses where, unlike H vs. H&H*, each hypothesis makes some contingent claim that the other doesn't, so that neither is entailed by the other? How do we determine which is more complex? What we need is some way to determine the degree of complexity in these cases—some way, in principle, to count or compare the number of entities and kinds of entities posited by different hypotheses. And we must make sure that we are comparing the number of simple, basic, or "atomic" entities (entities that are not made up of other entities), or make sure in some other way that we are comparing items of more or less equal complexity in one theory and the other. Otherwise, we might compare some items in one theory with more complex items in the other, and so come to wrong conclusions about which theory is more complex, and to what extent.

But if we manage to do this, then the more complex hypothesis will be less probable, other things being equal, than the simpler one, for roughly the same reason that H&H* is less probable than H: there are more ways it can go wrong.[3]

The real world hypothesis (RWH)

According to the real world hypothesis (RWH), there exists a mind-independent world of relatively stable, three-dimensional objects (including our own bodies), persisting through time, and generally capable of changing their positions and orientations; and a world in which these objects and bodies can interact in various ways—a world that at least approximates, in its spatial aspects, what we commonsensically take it to be. This is compatible with its turning out that the world is very strange or at odds with common sense in various ways. Perhaps, for example, there is no such thing as color in the world that in any way resembles our sensory experience. Perhaps physicists are right that the structure of space or the entities that occupy it, at the very small and very large scale, are strikingly non-commonsensical. But this seems compatible with RWH. While I may not be sure of the nature of the ultimate constituents of the table on which my computer sits, and why the table has the causal properties that it does, this is all compatible with the view that the table has an approximately square top, that it typically does not allow ordinary objects to fall through it, that it is larger and heavier than this book, that it can be moved, that it is made of wood, that it has four legs, and so on.

RWH seems to provide an excellent explanation of various regularities in experience, one that achieves a good combination of explanatory power and simplicity. Let us consider a few of these experiential regularities. Consider the fact that various features of your experience remain more or less constant or consistent. I presently have the experience as of sitting in a large armchair, with a matching ottoman that is roughly cubical in shape, a large bed to my right, windows behind it, and gently swaying trees in the distance outside. As I continue to have the apparent tactile and proprioceptive experiences characteristic of sitting on a soft surface, with legs stretched out and apparently supported by another soft surface, I notice that I also continue to have visual experiences as of sitting here: there visually appears to me to be a body sitting on a chair, with legs stretched out over an ottoman. And as I continue to have the apparent experience of moving my hands and fingers, I also have the visual experience of two hands moving and tapping away at the keys on a computer before me. I also seem to see words appear on a screen in front of me—just the words that I intend to write, and just the words that I seem to be typing on the keyboard. As I seem to look around, I seem to see the ottoman still there, holding up my feet; I seem to see a bed still to my right, windows beyond, and trees swaying gently beyond them.

As I seem to get up and move around in this room, the appearances persist, changing in ways that are consistent with apparent changes in my body's position as judged by my kinesthetic or proprioceptive sensations. It is worthwhile paying some attention to specific features of our visual experiences that are so common but that we rarely take explicit notice of, features that on reflection are easily explained by the geometry of perspective: that various rectangular shapes in my visual field often simultaneously get larger or smaller as I approach or step back from what I take to be windows is explained by change in my distance from objects; that certain shapes (apparently of cars and people outside my window) move across my visual field is explained by motion perpendicular to the line of sight; other continuous changes can be accounted for by gradual change in orientation or direction of motion. And all these changes are, again, consistent with the apparent kinesthetic or proprioceptive experiences. There are also the apparent auditory experiences—the sound of the tapping of fingers on keys, the increase in the volume of sounds as I approach the open windows and of trees swaying in the wind.

These independent, visual, kinesthetic, tactile, and auditory experiences can be explained by the hypothesis that I am an embodied being, and that I am presently in a room containing a chair, a bed, an ottoman, a computer, windows, and so on—and, more generally, that I exist in an environment that corresponds, more or less, to the sort of environment I take myself to inhabit. The hypothesis seems to account for a number of repeated, and repeatable, patterns of experience.

Objections to abductivism

The abductivist strategy is controversial. Indeed, it seems that a great many epistemologists remain skeptical of it. The abductivist faces at least three very significant challenges: (1) objections against the claim that the best available explanation is likely to be true; (2) objections against the claim that the realist hypothesis is the best explanation; and (3) the objection that we rarely form beliefs about our experiences or mental states, let alone have a broad enough basis of such beliefs to justify the inference to an external world.

Objections to IBE

The first set of objections targets IBE or abduction itself, alleging that being the best explanation is not a good indication of truth or likelihood. According to one of the most popular objections against IBE, the best explanation might just be the "best of a bad lot" (van Fraasen 1989: 143). When we use or apply IBE we consider some set of potential explanations of some given data—explanations we ourselves have thought of, or that others have suggested to us—and select one of these in accordance with our criteria for theory selection (e.g., explanatory power and simplicity). We may succeed in selecting the best explanation of those that we have formulated or proposed, but what about the indefinitely many explanations that we haven't even considered? It is true of course that if we choose a best explanation, we cannot help but choose among those we consider, and perhaps in some cases we are pragmatically justified in so doing if action requires that we make some choice, but that does not imply that we are *epistemically* justified, or justified in a sense relevant to the aim of getting at the truth. We are not warranted in regarding the best of the *considered* explanations to be the best explanation unless we have prior or independent reasons to think that the best is among them. Even granting for sake of argument that the best of *all* explanations is more likely to be true than false, it doesn't follow that the best of the *considered* explanations is more likely to be true than false. Our "best explanation" may indeed be the best of those explanations that we have considered, but for all we know they might be the "best of a bad lot."

The obvious way to reply is to defend the claim that we do indeed have good reason to think it likely that the best explanation is among the ones we consider. In some cases, perhaps we do have good reason to trust this. If in the morning I attempt to start my car without success, there's a limited set of explanations. Perhaps the battery is dead, or the starter needs replacing— or perhaps, more seriously, there's something wrong with the engine such that it won't start. I might begin to rule out some of these possibilities and narrow down the source of the problem. Or if my car emits a clunky metallic sound whenever I turn to the right, I know that probably has to do with basic steering-axle-wheel structure, and so I can examine that structure to determine more precisely what the problem is. There are all sorts of potential explanations that I do not consider because I have prior knowledge that they are bad or extremely unlikely explanations. We have good reason to think that apparent difficulty breathing is a sign of some abnormal or unhealthy condition of the lungs, restriction of passages to the lungs, perhaps trouble with the heart or with blood circulation, or anxiety, but not, say, a sign of tooth decay or a skin condition. So it seems that we often do have prior reason to think that the best explanation is to be found in some relatively restricted set of explanations. Something similar applies in various other practical and scientific contexts.

There is a problem with these examples, however, in the context of abductivism. Given that the abductivist is attempting to justify accepting RWH, we cannot rely on background beliefs that assume that RWH is true. In the above examples, our reasons for restricting the class of explanations to consider do seem to depend on such background beliefs. The crucial question, then, is whether we can have prior reasons to believe that these restrictions are warranted, or that the best explanation is likely to be among the ones we consider—reasons that do not assume that RWH is true. If we have such reasons, it seems that they must be independent of empirical assumptions, and so must be *a priori*, or else we beg the question against the skeptic by assuming that we are already warranted in accepting RWH.

Do we have *a priori* reasons to think that RWH is the best of some *given* set of explanations but also of *all* possible explanations, and so—assuming that the best of all explanations is more likely to be true than not—that RWH is more likely to be true than not? We will be in a better position to answer this question after discussing the sorts of alternative explanations philosophers tend to consider in the context of responding to skepticism about the external world.

There is, however, another objection that targets IBE. In order to be epistemically justified in believing a hypothesis, it must minimally be more probable than its negation, more likely to be true than not. But then, it is not enough that it be more probable than *each* competing hypothesis: it must also be more probable than the *disjunction* of all competing hypotheses. To see this, suppose for simplicity that there are only seven possible explanations of the data of experience: RWH, and six competing skeptical alternatives to RWH. Suppose that these seven hypotheses exhaust the possibilities so that the probability is 1 that exactly one of these hypotheses is true. RWH might have a higher probability than each of its competitors if the competitors each have a probability of 0.1, for then RWH would have a probability of 0.4. But then, despite being the best explanation in the sense of being better than each alternative, we would not be justified in taking RWH to be more likely to be true than not. It seems that, in order to be justified, RWH must not only be better and so more likely than each competing hypothesis, but that it be better and so more likely than the *disjunction* of competing hypotheses. Let's accept this for now as an amendment of IBE, and consider its relevance to the justification of RWH after we have compared RWH and its competitors. Our question then will be: can the abductivist support the claim that RWH is not only better than each competitor, but better than the *disjunction* of competing hypotheses?

RWH vs. skeptical hypotheses

Some skeptics grant, for sake of argument at least, that IBE is a legitimate form of inference, but claim that abductivists go wrong in their application of IBE to the problem of the external world: they deny that we are justified in regarding RWH to be the best explanation, for they claim that there are other alternative explanations that are at least as good.

To see why the skeptic thinks that some skeptical hypotheses are strong competitors, including ones we have already considered in the very first chapter, it may help to begin by briefly considering some that are more clearly inferior. Suppose the skeptic asks you to consider the possibility that RWH is false, and that your experiences are all caused, say, by a flying spaghetti monster. Let's compare this to RWH. As we have already seen, RWH provides an explanation of various experiential regularities; it makes it more likely that I do undergo these experiential regularities. The claim that my experiences are caused somehow by the flying spaghetti monster says nothing about why I should expect to have one set of experiences rather than another, or why I should experience certain sorts of regularities rather than others or no identifiable regularity at all. The hypothesis thus fails to provide much *explanatory power*—very little, if anything, of the ultimate experiential data or experiential evidence would be explained by the truth of this hypothesis. The skeptic could of course build into the hypothesis that the flying spaghetti monster *causes you to have just the experiences, or patterns of experience, that you do in fact have*, but the advantage gained is illusory: the hypothesis still tells us nothing about why we experience what we do in fact experience, or if it does, it merely raises a parallel question at another level: why does the spaghetti monster cause us to experience what we do in fact experience? We might grant for sake of argument that it is *possible* that the spaghetti monster does cause this experience, but we need to know something about the details, about how or why the spaghetti monster influences our experiences, in order to compare its explanatory power and simplicity to RWH.

But let's suppose that the skeptic does provide us some of these details. Indeed, let's suppose that the account provided is at least roughly along the lines of one of Descartes' famous skeptical hypotheses: there exists a flying spaghetti monster *who intends to deceive us into believing that RWH is true*. This would better explain why we have some of the experiential regularities that we do, for we then have a reason why this monster would cause these experiential regularities: it is in virtue of these experiential regularities that we believe RWH, so it would make sense that a flying spaghetti monster intent on deceiving us into believing RWH would cause these experiences in us.

There's a second respect in which this hypothesis is inferior. There's a clear sense in which the hypothesis is more complex than it needs to be: why does it matter that the cause of our delusive experiences is a *flying spaghetti monster*? That element of the skeptical hypothesis seems to play no role in accounting for the experiences we have. We have no loss of explanatory power when we replace the claim that there is a flying spaghetti monster with the claim that there is some being or other—whether it be God, an evil genius, some alien, or a flying spaghetti monster—intent on deceiving us into believing RWH. What matters is that the entity in question be capable of producing the relevant experience. It is no surprise, then, that something like Descartes' evil genius hypothesis has been such a popular skeptical hypothesis: it seems to do the explanatory work of the RWH at minimum cost in terms of complexity of the hypothesis.

How does RWH compare to the evil genius hypothesis? Initially, it might seem that this skeptical hypothesis is superior, for while such a hypothesis posits very few entities—the mind of the deceiver, the mind of the victim, and the mental states, ideas, and experiences of each—RWH is committed to more (see, e.g., Vogel 1990: 662; Fumerton 2005: 95). But if RWH invokes spatial objects with movable parts to explain certain patterns of experience, then each of these movable parts will have their corresponding items (ideas) in the skeptical alternative. The skeptical hypothesis requires discrete ideas that correspond to all the discrete objects, parts, and processes that have an explanatory role in RWH. If the addition of objects in RWH makes for greater complexity, there is no clear reason why the deceiver's ideas or mental states which represent these objects do not make for greater complexity as well.

Now, in addition to these items, the evil genius hypothesis must posit the existence of a powerful conscious being with a persistent intention to deceive us into believing in RWH. This hypothesis thus seems more complex. But does this really add complexity? Perhaps it is God who causes this experience, where God is a *necessary* being. The existence of this being is not a contingent matter, and so the skeptical hypothesis does not posit the existence of more *contingent* beings than the RWH. However, even granting that the existence of God is a non-contingent matter, that alone doesn't help us determine whether the existence of God is (necessarily) true or false. It therefore still amounts to an additional claim, one that exposes us to additional risk, that such a being exists, and it doesn't seem that we are committed to any such additional entity in positing the existence of various objects. We don't need to posit, in addition to that, some being that is partly constituted by such objects.

But perhaps there is a good reason to think that such a being—a necessary being—exists. Even so, there is another difficulty with this skeptical hypothesis, for it posits a being with *a persistent intention to deceive*. There is nothing in RWH that corresponds to this persistent intention to deceive.

It is time to return to the problems discussed in the previous section. The first question was: Do we have *a priori* reasons to think that RWH is the best of some *given* set of explanations but also of *all* possible explanations, and so—assuming that the best of all explanations is more likely to be true than not—that RWH is more likely to be true than not? Well, aside from hypotheses like the evil genius hypothesis, do we have good reasons to think that there are other alternative hypotheses that compete with RWH? Do we have good reasons to think there are hypotheses that are better than the evil genius hypotheses and in competition with RWH? It is actually very difficult to come up with any such hypotheses—so difficult, in fact, that one might doubt that any superior hypothesis exists. Let's distinguish the hypotheses that compete with RWH into two sorts: those that attempt to achieve a comparable combination of explanatory power and simplicity by (i) positing the existence of *spatial properties like those of RWH*, or (ii) by positing some *radically different* properties (whether they be spatial or non-spatial).[4] If they are of kind (i) then it is difficult to see how they will achieve a comparable combination of explanatory power and simplicity and yet remain *skeptical* hypotheses. The point, to put it in a suggestive but admittedly vague manner, is that spheres behave like spheres, and cubes behave like cubes, and only behave otherwise if there is some distorting mechanism or process that adds complexity to the system.[5] If the hypotheses are of kind (ii), then the only way they can compete with RWH is if they mimic spatial properties very closely, and it seems that the only hypotheses of this sort are those that involve *models or representations of* a world of the RWH sort. But then, we are back to the evil genius hypothesis and others of the same sort, and these end up being more complex, as we have seen. So it seems that we do have good, prior reason to suppose that RWH is better than *all* alternative skeptical hypotheses, and not just better than those we explicitly consider.

What about the second problem: can the abductivist support the claim that RWH is not only better than each competitor, but better than the *disjunction* of competing hypotheses? This is a serious problem, and one that is difficult to tackle without moving into very technical territory. But here too there is something intuitive to say. Suppose that H1 makes more specific predications than H2, in roughly the way that the hypothesis that I am reading a book makes more specific predictions about my experiences than the hypothesis that I am dreaming. Then, not only is H1 more probable, other things being equal, than H2, but H1 becomes more and more probable than H2 as more data that H1 predicts come in, just as the hypothesis that I am reading a book becomes more and more probable than the hypothesis that I am dreaming the more experiences of reading a book I have. When it comes to RWH, the data we have accumulated and continue to accumulate that RWH makes highly likely is immense. It is plausible to think that this makes RWH a *great deal* more probable than the alternative skeptical hypotheses.

One worry with this intuitive line of reasoning is that there may be a number of skeptical hypotheses that have a comparable degree of explanatory power, and even if the arguments of this section do establish that they are bound to be more complex, it is not clear that they will be so much more complex that RWH will be significantly more probable than each, so much so that it is more probable than their disjunction. The concern might thus remain, though perhaps there is room to resist it.

The abductivist might also respond that the objection assumes that we must distribute the probabilities so that there are indefinitely many alternative skeptical hypotheses, and only one realist hypothesis. While there is a sense in which there are indefinitely many skeptical hypotheses (dream hypothesis, BIV-hypothesis, deceiving God hypothesis, deceiving alien hypothesis, deceiving super-duper neurosurgeon hypothesis, deceiving spaghetti-monster hypothesis...?), there might be good reason to think that we are really comparing *types* of hypotheses, and that there are actually only a few hypothesis *types* that have competing explanatory virtues that are worth considering. For example, in line with the arguments given above, perhaps only skeptical hypotheses that invoke powerful deceivers could have the combination of explanatory power and simplicity that is in the vicinity of the RWH. If that is so, the RWH might still turn out to be far better than these alternatives to make it plausible that it is more probable than the disjunction of alternatives.

The problem of scarcity of basic beliefs

According to the traditional view that I have called mental state foundationalism (MSF), only beliefs about given properties or features of experience are empirically foundational; external world beliefs would have to ultimately depend for their justification on these foundational beliefs. This traditional view faces what we might call the scarcity objection, according to which such foundational beliefs are too few and far between to provide adequate support for an abductive inference to the external world.

The objection is straightforward:[6] We rarely have beliefs about our own experiences, sensations, apparent memories, or the contents of our own mental states. Therefore, such beliefs fail to constitute a sufficient empirical foundation for perceptual knowledge or justified belief. In support of the claim that we rarely have beliefs about the contents of our own experiences, Pollock and Cruz (1999) argue (a) that we are normally unaware of having thoughts about experiences, and (b) that if we are normally unaware of having such thoughts, then, other things being equal, it is reasonable to think that we do not in fact have them, and so do not have the corresponding beliefs.

Pollock is also concerned that, even if we grant for the sake of argument that there are many beliefs about our experiences, our ordinary perceptual beliefs are rarely *based* on beliefs about experiences, for we normally "move directly from our percepts [or perceptual experiences] to our beliefs about the world, without going through intermediary beliefs about how things appear to us" (2001: 44). Granted, nothing in classical foundationalism or MSF requires that we literally "go through intermediary beliefs" successively in time; basic and non-basic beliefs may be held simultaneously. Even so, we rarely seem to hold ordinary beliefs on the basis of intermediary beliefs about what is given in experience.

It is not clear how serious these concerns are, for even if we rarely form such beliefs, perhaps there is a sense in which they are readily available to us by reflection alone. We might still have good reasons for belief in the external world, even if we don't base our beliefs on the good reasons we have. But the problem for MSF becomes more serious if we think that ordinary subjects, including philosophers, don't have a very developed ability to describe or conceptualize the experiential features and regularities that the abductivist is attempting to explain. We inevitably resort, as I have above, to describing our experiences at least partly in terms of physical objects we associate with them, and in rather general and suggestive terms, but it takes a great deal of attention and care, and a developed skill, to adequately conceptualize the qualitative features of even a very narrow range of experiences. Moreover, this ability apparently varies a great deal between different subjects; some are much better at conceptualizing and describing specific patterns of spatial properties in experience than others, and it seems odd to suggest that they have stronger justification for external world beliefs because of that. Thus, not only do we have few beliefs regarding our own experiences of the sort that the MSF abductivist apparently requires, but many of us lack a robust ability to form such beliefs about patterns of experience.[7]

Suppose that, under the pressure of this objection, we grant that we rarely have beliefs about what is given in experience. Can we still hold on to abductivism? Well, we might hold that having beliefs about our experiences is not required for having justified beliefs about the external world, and yet that these experiences can still play an epistemic role, even for the abductivist.[8] After all, it is the experiences themselves that we are trying to explain, experiences to which we have a direct or conscious access, and if these experiences can justify beliefs about mental states without first needing to be conceptualized or described in some way, then why can't they be relevant to the justification of external world beliefs without such conceptualization? One worry is that the subjects would need to be able to grasp that their experiences are best explained by external world objects, and, as we have seen, that grasp seems to require noticing that we have particular patterns or regularities in experience, not just noticing one momentary experience or appearance. But again, why should noticing these patterns require having detailed beliefs about our experiences? As BonJour (2007) tentatively suggests, it is natural to take ordinary subjects to notice such patterns in experience regularly, and to tacitly understand that certain sorts of objects explain why they have *these* experiences rather than others. The requirement that we hold beliefs about our experiences, or that we infer to the best explanation in explicit ways, might be a sign of over-intellectualization—perhaps a case of confusing the philosopher's position, which requires articulating the justification we might have for our beliefs, with the justified subject's position, which requires having justification, and being able to grasp what it involves in at least a tacit and approximate way. It is not yet clear that such an attempt to combine EWF with abductivism is defensible, but it seems to be a possibility worth investigating.

1 Can you think of an example, either from a scientific context or ordinary practical context, of a pair of competing hypotheses that are more or less equal in terms of explanatory power or their ability to account for what is experienced, but where one is preferred over the other due to its relative simplicity? Can you think of a pair of competing hypotheses that are more or less equal in terms of simplicity, but where one is better in terms of explanatory power?

2 Consider the hypothesis that your life has, at least for a few years now, been an extended coherent dream created by your sub-conscious, or that your brain has recently been hooked to a virtual reality or "experience machine" while you were asleep. Would that be an inferior explanation of your present experiences? Why? What is it about this hypothesis that makes it inferior to the RWH?

3 At least some of our experiences lead more or less automatically to specific beliefs, though we find it difficult to explain what it is about these experiences that lead us to form the beliefs. For example, we may recognize friends or acquaintances by looking at their faces, and notice if they are angry, sad, or confused, by their facial expressions. Can you think of other examples of this sort? How extensive is this inability to describe the relevant experienced features? Is this a problem for the abductivist approach?

Locke provides an early version of what looks like an abductivist argument against skepticism about the external world in his *Essay Concerning Human Understanding* (1690: Bk.IV.Ch.xi). For recent attempts to respond to skepticism via IBE, see Vogel's papers on the subject: "Cartesian Skepticism and Inference to the Best Explanation" (1990); "Internalist Responses to Skepticism" (2008), and the exchange between Vogel and Fumerton on whether skepticism can be refuted (in Steup and Sosa 2005). See also BonJour's "Foundationalism and the External World" (1999), McCain's *Evidentialism and Epistemic Justification* (2014: Ch. 6), and Huemer's "Serious Theories and Skeptical Theories: Why You are Probably Not a Brain in a Vat" (2016).

Douven's *Stanford Encyclopedia of Philosophy* entry on "abductivism" provides an introduction to abduction or IBE with connections to philosophy of science, including a brief survey of famous criticisms from van Fraasen (1989), and a section on the relation between IBE and probability. A great, book-length discussion of IBE is provided by Lipton in his *Inference to the Best Explanation* (2004).

For attempts to combine abductive responses to skepticism with external world foundationalism, see BonJour's "Are Perceptual Beliefs Properly Basic?" (2007) and Moser's *Knowledge and Evidence* (1989: esp 158–64).

7

Phenomenal conservatism

We turn in this chapter to one of the most prominent forms of external world foundationalism (EWF), phenomenal conservatism or dogmatism. According to this view, perceptual "seemings" or appearances can be a source of foundational justification for external world beliefs. The view is intuitively appealing, seems to satisfy a broadly internalist requirement, and sidesteps the worries with the coherentist and foundationalist alternatives discussed in previous chapters: it gives perceptual experiences or appearances a central role, and avoids skeptical consequences quite easily. We discuss the nature of seemings and whether their nature suits them well for the epistemic role assigned to them, and then briefly consider some objections to the view: that it makes attaining perceptual justification *too easy*, that it conflicts with good probabilistic reasoning, and that it conflicts with the intuition that other mental states can influence the epistemic efficacy of seemings. We also briefly consider whether phenomenal conservatism has trouble accommodating the justification of *introspective* beliefs. We end by asking whether phenomenal conservatism can be regarded as a form of access internalism, and raising the worry that it severs the connection between epistemic justification and the truth or probability of one's beliefs.

Internalist alternatives to mental state foundationalism (MSF)

According to mental state foundationalism (MSF), the only empirically justified foundational beliefs are beliefs about our own mental states; empirical beliefs about the external world are justified inferentially, if at all. As we observed in the previous chapter, the challenge of avoiding skepticism about the external world is serious for MSF. A view that allows for the foundational justification of empirical beliefs about extra-mental entities might have better resources for avoiding skepticism; a view that includes beliefs about the external world in this set would seem to avoid these difficulties quite easily. But in virtue of what are these beliefs justified? And are such views defensible?

Consider, for example, a view once defended by Roderick Chisholm (1980) that is often called "epistemic conservatism," and sometimes, more aptly, "doxastic conservatism." The doxastic conservative takes the mere fact that you believe some proposition *P* to provide *prima facie* justification for believing that *P*. This view does not imply that the mere fact that you believe something renders the belief justified, for it may be that your belief is *prima facie* justified but not *ultima facie* justified: if you have good reasons to disbelieve that *P*, or good reasons to think that your belief that *P* is unreliable or untrustworthy, then your belief is "defeated" and not justified. In other words:

DC: If *S* believes that *P* then, in the *absence of defeaters*, S has some degree of justification for believing that *P*.

Doxastic conservatism may seem to inherit some of the problems we raised against coherentism about justification. There is the isolation problem: why should the mere fact that one believes something provide any reason or assurance that the belief is true, or that it corresponds in any way to reality? One's belief might be "isolated" from reality, and isolated from any observations or sensory input that would connect that belief to reality. Doxastic conservatism also seems vulnerable to the *alternative systems objection*. There are indefinitely many alternative sets of belief that one might hold, and most of these will fail to represent or correspond to reality. The underlying worry of both objections is that epistemically justified beliefs must be probable, truth-conducive, or indicative of truth in some way, but the mere fact that we hold some undefeated beliefs fails to satisfy this requirement.

Unlike doxastic conservatism, other forms of foundationalism can allow experiences to play a justificatory role. These experiences serve to "anchor" our beliefs to or keep them from being totally isolated from reality; and they provide a crucial constraint on the contents of our beliefs. Thus, the epistemic role assigned to experience or observation seems to block the isolation objection and the alternative systems objection. Indeed, it seems that this problem with doxastic conservatism is the same as the one raised for coherentism: it fails to assign an epistemic role to experience or observation.

Perhaps the doxastic conservative can, like the coherentist, assign a special role for beliefs that are experiential or observational in the broad sense of being casually (but not epistemically) based on experience or observation. And perhaps this can be done in a motivated, non-*ad hoc* way: if the mere fact that I believe something provides some justification, then perhaps the more strongly I believe it, or the higher my degree of confidence in the belief, the higher my justification for it. Experiential beliefs tend to be held with a great deal of confidence, and so will tend to have a particularly high degree of justification, absent defeaters. Still, it seems *possible*, in principle, for one to have a high degree of confidence in beliefs that are isolated from any experiential or perceptual input, and that are not supported by any arguments or inferences. If these beliefs count as epistemically justified then aren't we giving up the requirement that these beliefs be truth-conductive, that they be connected to truth or probability?

Aside from this abstract and general worry about truth-conduciveness, there's the worry that the view is vulnerable to particular counterexamples. We can begin by considering an extreme example of a case of "isolation" of beliefs from underlying experiences.[1] Suppose that I enter into some strange state of shock as a result of looking down while climbing a mountain, and that as a result my mind becomes fixed on elaborate beliefs about being stuck on the mountain even after my friends rescue me. Suppose that in the attempt to shake me out of my state, my friends take me to a symphony, and suppose that I am indeed experiencing just the sort of experience normally produced by one's going to the symphony. Normally, having such experiences would generate other beliefs about my environment, and these would conflict with my beliefs about being on a mountain. But suppose none of this is happening, and that my beliefs are utterly unaffected by the experiences. If we allow for this possibility, then the doxastic conservative will have to accept the counterintuitive implication that my mountain-climbing beliefs are epistemically justified. The doxastic conservative might reply by providing an "error theory" to explain why we might find this reaction intuitive: perhaps we mistakenly take these beliefs to be unjustified merely because it is difficult for us to imagine not having any beliefs that are affected by our sensory experiences, and so, difficult for us to imagine my having no beliefs that defeat my mountain-climbing beliefs.

Perhaps better counterexamples are provided by cases in which one forms a belief in a proposition one has no evidence for or against. Suppose that despite lacking any evidence for or against the belief, I somehow come to believe that there is an even number of grains of sand on a particular beach (Foley 1983: 174–5), or that a particular coin that is tossed and lands out of sight has landed 'tails' up (Christensen 1994: 74). Suppose I lack any defeaters for the belief. Unlike the above case, we don't have to imagine here that my beliefs are utterly unaffected by my experiences. It is true that most ordinary subjects know that such beliefs are unreliable, and we tend to assume that subjects would therefore have good defeaters for such beliefs. Nevertheless, it is not difficult to imagine or conceive of such a case. Doxastic conservatism yields the counterintuitive result that this belief is justified.[2]

Phenomenal conservatism and dogmatism

There are alternative accounts that also allow for a broader base of basic or foundationally justified belief as compared to MSF, but that do not take the mere fact that one believes that *P* to provide justification. According to *phenomenal conservatism* (PC), a kind of non-belief state can provide justification:

> PC: If it *seems* or *appears* to *S* that *P* then, in the absence of defeaters, *S* thereby has some degree of justification for believing that *P*.[3]

Phenomenal conservatives typically hold that seemings come in various sorts: perceptual, introspective, memorial, and intellectual or intuitive. This same view is sometimes called *dogmatism*, though often this label is used to refer specifically to the view that *perceptual* seemings are a source of justification:[4]

> DOG: If it *perceptually seems* or *perceptually appears* to *S* that *P*, then, in the absence of defeaters, *S* thereby has some justification for believing that *P*.

PC implies DOG, but DOG does not imply PC. However, in what follows I will discuss the more general view of phenomenal conservatism, as it provides a more complete account of justification, though as usual we focus on perception and beliefs about the external world.

Phenomenal conservatives typically claim that accepting PC allows them to treat a wide range of beliefs as epistemically justified—indeed, as basic. For example, I believe that I am sitting by a fire, that I chopped some wood earlier, that I feel warm, that I am thinking about putting more wood on the fire, that wood comes from trees, that three is greater than two, that circles have no corners, and that pain is intrinsically bad. It is plausible to say that I believe these propositions because that's how things appear or seem to me— because it seems to me that I am sitting by the fire, that I chopped wood earlier, that I feel warm, and so on. If I do indeed believe these things on the basis of these seemings or appearances, and they constitute an adequate source of justification, then, in the absence of defeaters, the corresponding beliefs are justified to some degree. One way that phenomenal conservatives have defended their view is by arguing that the denial of PC leads to radical skepticism. As we have already seen, anyone who denies that some external world beliefs can be foundationally justified faces some serious challenges in attempting to account for justified belief in the external world. Phenomenal conservatives sometimes also claim that PC itself is intuitive: beliefs that are based on appearances or seemings, like the above, *seem* to be justified! Is it not intuitive that its perceptually seeming to me that I am sitting by the fire provides, in the absence of defeaters, some justification for believing that I am indeed sitting by the fire?

Skepticism and epistemological methodology

This is a good point to discuss an important matter of methodology that is related to the first way mentioned above that alternatives to MSF are motivated. Should the fact that a particular view about the source or nature of justification has skeptical consequences, or the fact that it avoids skeptical consequences, be relevant to its evaluation? Is the fact that a view would avoid some form of skepticism, if true, a good reason to accept it as true? Let us first ask a different or less ambiguous question: are we justified in accepting such a view *merely* because we *like* the non-skeptical result? Surely not—at least not if our aim is to accept *true* epistemological views and avoid *false* ones. Perhaps it is sometimes good to accept a view that more easily avoids skepticism for the sake of the psychological effects this would have, or for other pragmatic or moral considerations. Even if there is something to this, that would not be directly relevant to an evaluation of the *truth* of these epistemological views. If we really are concerned with the *truth* of our epistemological positions, then the fact that a view would avoid skepticism, if true, would be a good reason to accept it only if we had some prior reason to think that skepticism is false. But then, the interesting and central issue is just what prior reasons we have to take skepticism to be false.

The advocate of PC might accept all of this. While they and others might motivate their respective views on the basis of the claim that their views avoid skepticism if true, this might be understood as a dialectical strategy aimed at persuasion: an attempt to get others who are interested in avoiding skepticism to consider the proposed view more seriously. They might nevertheless agree that we should not accept an epistemological position *merely* because it would allow us to avoid a skeptical result we really don't like; they might insist that we do have good reasons to deny skepticism.

There is a second, related point about methodology. None of this is to say that we don't already have good reasons to deny skepticism. (But nor is it to affirm that we do have good reasons to deny skepticism.) Perhaps, as G. E. Moore (1959) and others seem to have thought, it is obvious that we do know that we have hands, and can competently infer that skepticism about whether we have hands must be false, and that any skeptical argument with a contrary conclusion must be mistaken, have some false premise or assumption, or rely on some fallacious reasoning. But even *if* this is right, the philosophically interesting task is to articulate how we could know this, and on what basis. Where exactly do the skeptical arguments go wrong? Why is this "obviousness" epistemologically legitimate and not merely psychological? The answer to *these* questions are not obvious, and carrying out the task of answering them seriously and in an intellectually or philosophically satisfying way is very difficult. As we discussed in the chapter introducing contemporary debates in epistemology, we take skepticism seriously in order to better understand what makes knowledge and justification possible, and to determine the extent or scope of our knowledge and justification, in a philosophically and intellectually satisfying way.

The nature of seemings

Returning now to phenomenal conservatism: what are "seemings" or "appearances"? It is difficult to find any proponent of PC offering a strict definition or analysis of seemings. The distinction between seemings and beliefs is typically introduced with examples. Some of the best examples are perceptual or sensory ones: we have all experienced various optical or visual illusions, and very often, even after we realize they are only illusions, the misleading seemings or appearances persist. Once I discovered that a stick merely looks or appears bent or broken when partly submerged in water, I no longer believe that it is bent. It still *seems* that the stick is bent, even though I do not believe that it is. It also still seems to me that Euclid's parallel postulate (that parallel lines never meet no matter how far they are extended) is necessarily true, even after learning about the consistency of non-Euclidean geometries that conflict with it. Perhaps sometimes our realization that an appearance is false makes it disappear, but very often our sensory, intuitive, and memorial seemings or appearances persist after the realization that they are false. A seeming that *P* is thus distinct from the belief that *P*.

Phenomenal conservatives typically also claim that seemings cannot be identified with dispositions, inclinations, or impulses to believe. Michael Huemer (2007: 30–1) has argued for this on three main grounds. First, it is possible to have a persisting seeming or appearance but be so convinced that it is a mere illusion that one has no disposition or inclination at all to believe it. We might naturally worry that there's always *some* inclination to believe in such cases, however suppressed or weakened it is. Still, it's worth noting that a very *strong or forceful* seeming often persists, and it doesn't make sense to identify this with a *mild* inclination to believe. Second, it is possible to be inclined to believe that *P* (because, e.g., you really want it to be true) in the absence of a corresponding seeming that *P*. Third, appearances can provide non-trivial explanations for what we believe or what we are disposed to believe: I am inclined to believe that there is a bus approaching because it perceptually seems that there is; understanding the latter seeming as an inclination to believe trivializes the explanation. Proponents of phenomenal conservatism thus typically hold that seemings are distinct from beliefs and inclinations to believe. The phenomenal conservative need not deny that we sometimes use the term "it seems to me that ..." to mean something like "I'm inclined to believe that ...," but they claim that there is another, central sense of the term that is appropriate and epistemically relevant.

Phenomenal conservatives do take seemings to be like beliefs in that they are propositional attitudes or at least have propositional contents—they are seemings *that so-and-so*. And they hold that seemings have a distinctive, familiar, though difficult to describe phenomenal character: seemings are "assertive" (Huemer 2013); they have a "phenomenal force" to them such that "it 'feels as if' we can just tell that those propositions are true...just by virtue of having them so represented" (Pryor 2000: 547, n.23); "a seeming that P 'recommends' P as true or 'assures' the subject of P's truth" (Tucker 2013: 6).

Some still worry that there really isn't such a thing as a seeming that is propositional and yet distinct from something like a conscious inclination or impulse to believe something. To motivate this, consider the case of illusions like that of the stick-in-water. In such a case, I am conscious of certain detailed visual sensations and, as a result, may have some impulse to believe that the stick is bent. If I am fully convinced it is an illusion I will have little or no inclination to believe that the stick is bent, and yet I can't deny that there's a sense in which it very much *looks* or *seems* to be bent. Perhaps what is happening is this: I notice certain features or qualities of sense data, or of my experiences, features that I normally take to be strongly indicative of the presence of a bent stick, features that would lead me to so believe if I did not know better. It is undeniable that these phenomenal qualities or features persist, and it is natural to describe this by saying, "it still seems to me that the stick is bent, even though it obviously isn't."

This might suggest the following contrasting view of seemings as a more complex kind of inclination to believe.[5] Sometimes we do use the term "it seems that P" to mean, simply, "I'm inclined to believe that P." But in many other cases, including the main examples the phenomenal conservative appeals to, we say that "it seems to S that P" when S is aware or conscious of something (e.g., a sense datum, experience, or quality of this sense datum or experience), and S is inclined to take it to be normally or usually indicative of the truth of P. We can thus agree with the phenomenal conservative that a seeming that P is not, in these cases, to be identified with a mere inclination to believe that P. I might be inclined to believe, say, that I am in good health merely because I want to believe it, but it doesn't follow that it seems to me that I am in good health. We can also agree that a seeming that P need not involve one's having an inclination to believe that P at all: it involves being inclined to take something to be normally indicative of the truth of P, though one might not take the given situation to be normal. Moreover, we avoid the trivialization worry: I am inclined to believe that a bus is approaching because I am aware of sensory features (not propositional seemings) that I am strongly inclined to take to be a good or reliable indicator of such things. This alternative account is thus apparently able to avoid the difficulties Huemer raised with the view that a seeming that P can be identified with an inclination to believe that P.

This is not an account of seemings that the phenomenal conservative should be happy to accept, for it threatens an epistemic regress. If the belief that P is justified by a seeming that P, but this is understood as an inclination to take some experience or experiential feature as indicative of the truth of P, then it makes sense to ask what justifies taking the experience to be indicative of the truth. So, far from being the suitable justifier that itself requires no justification, the seeming that P is itself a belief or belief-like state that requires justification.

Many phenomenal conservatives and dogmatists will deny that an account of seemings along the lines just offered is adequate, preferring to treat seemings as a special kind of propositional attitude, distinct from fears and hopes, as well as beliefs and inclinations to believe of various kinds. Let us grant this for now.

Objections to phenomenal conservatism

The problem of easy knowledge

In the previous two chapters we discussed epistemological views that, in certain respects, seem to make the acquisition or possession of epistemic justification rather difficult. Internalist coherentism seems to make epistemic justification impossible, while abductivism faces serious objections in the attempt to justify explanatory inference and its application to the problem of the external world. Phenomenal conservatism and dogmatism seem to avoid such difficulties. But many are dissatisfied with these views, claiming that they have all the advantages of "theft over honest toil." Phenomenal conservatism, the complaint goes, makes the acquisition of justification and the response to skepticism *much too easy.*

How can we clarify and motivate this concern? One way to do so is the "problem of easy knowledge," which was initially presented as a problem for knowledge, though we here focus on the parallel problem for epistemic justification.[6] The problem comes in two forms.

The first version of the problem of easy knowledge involves cases of deductive closure. To use Cohen's (2002) famous example, suppose that I want to acquire a red table for my new home. Suppose that I find a particular table that seems red to me. If phenomenal conservatism is true, then I can arrive at knowledge, or at least justified belief, by the following simple inference:

1   This table is red. (Formed on the basis of a perceptual seeming that the table is red.)

2   If this table is red then it is not a white table illuminated by red lights.

3   So, this table is not a white table illuminated by red lights.

The same goes for the following inference:

1   I have a hand. (Formed on the basis of a perceptual seeming that I have a hand.)

2   If I have a hand, then I am not a handless brain in a vat caused to have a perceptual seeming of a hand.

3   So, I am not a handless brain in a vat caused to have a perceptual seeming of a hand.

The problem is that it seems implausible that I could acquire justification for the belief that the table is not a white table illuminated by red lights *merely* on the basis of its seeming to me that it is red. Of course, I normally do have independent reasons to trust that the tables I see have the colors they seem to have. But according to phenomenal conservatism, a seeming that *P* is good enough on its own, absent defeaters, to provide justification for the belief that *P*—no background needed! But that seems implausible. We can even imagine other, similar cases where the background knowledge is lacking, and the subject lacks defeaters, but is intuitively unjustified.[7] Similarly, it is implausible that I could acquire justification for the belief that I am not a brain in a vat that merely seems to have hands on the basis of its seeming to me that I have hands.

Is there a way for the phenomenal conservative to block the argument? It is difficult to see how. Let's make this explicit: suppose that in each case (1) is indeed non-inferentially justified for me on the basis of the corresponding seeming or appearance, that I know the obvious entailment (2) *a priori*, and that on the basis of this I infer (3). Suppose also that we accept the following intuitively plausible principle of closure: if *S* is justified in believing that *P*, knows that P entails Q, and infers on the basis of this that Q, then S is justified in believing that Q. (This is a principle that phenomenal conservatives and dogmatists tend to accept.) It then follows that I am justified in believing (3). The objector takes the lesson here to be that mere seemings cannot provide justification. Justification can't be that easy.

The problem of easy knowledge (or easy justification) comes in a second form as well: phenomenal conservatism allows one to acquire justification in the reliability of one's perceptual seemings or perceptual experiences in an epistemically circular way. If phenomenal conservatism is true, then I can arrive at knowledge or at least justified belief in the reliability of my perceptual seemings (or other sorts of seemings) in the following way:

1 P. (Formed on the basis of a perceptual seeming)

2 It seems to me that P. (Formed on the basis of an introspective seeming)

3 Q. (Formed on the basis of a perceptual seeming)

4 It seems to me that Q. (Formed on the basis of an introspective seeming)

   etc...

5 Therefore, most of my perceptual seemings are true.

Given some plausible principle of justification by induction, I can infer from the premises that my perceptual seemings are (probably) reliable. The problem is that it is intuitively implausible that I could come to acquire justification for the reliability of my seemings by relying on the very seemings whose reliability one is attempting to justify. But it's not clear how the phenomenal conservative can deny that this is a legitimate way to acquire justification for the reliability of one's seemings.

One possible reply is to grant that such arguments are question-begging and epistemically useless if presented to someone who doubts the relia-bility or trustworthiness of such seemings, but hold that it can still provide a subject who lacks that doubt with justification. While the argument is question-begging against the skeptic, that is no reason to deny that one could, in the absence of defeaters, acquire knowledge or justification on the basis of such arguments (Pryor 2004; Markie 2005). However, some object that such arguments remain intuitively problematic, whether or not they are dialectically question-begging (Cohen 2005).

The objection from evidential probability

A very closely related worry, sometimes called the Bayesian objection to dogmatism or phenomenal conservatism, is that the view is in conflict with good probabilistic reasoning. Suppose that its seeming to me that the table is red can count on its own as evidence that raises the probability of the proposition that it is red. Doesn't it also count as evidence for and so raise the probability of the proposition that *the table is white but illuminated so as to seem red*? (Call this hypothesis *W*.) After all, the truth of *W* would make likely (indeed, entail) that it seems red, and so (in line with Bayesianism) given the evidence that the table seems red, the probability of *W* goes up, and so the probability of *not-W* should go down. But how could evidence that makes the probability of a proposition go down provide positive justification for believing that very proposition? Surely it could not.[8]

There have been a handful of recent responses to this probabilistic objection.[9] One response is to point out that phenomenal conservatism requires only that one have the relevant seemings or appearances, not that one have access to the fact that one has them. The objection treats the fact that one has certain seemings as evidence, and so as something one has some sort of access to, but phenomenal conservatism denies that access to the fact that one has such-and-such seemings is the only way that seemings can make a difference to justification. What justifies treating cases where the subject has no such access and cases where the subject does have it similarly? White (2006: 534–5) argues that what is a rational or justified response to appearances for the subject who reflects explicitly on his or her appearances is surely also a rational or justified response for the unreflecting subject with the same appearances. But one may reasonably question whether this is right.[10] After all, a failure to notice or observe something can make a difference to justification: if you do something wrong in my presence, but I don't notice, that doesn't justify me in blaming you; analogously, why can't a failure to notice or reflect on something in my own mind make it rational for me to believe something, though reflecting on it might change that. Other, more technical responses question the adequacy of the classical formal apparatus of Bayesian probability theory, or its standard interpretation, to model epistemic justification. They thus attempt to show that the problem may lie with classical (Bayesian) probability theory rather than with dogmatism or phenomenal conservatism.[11]

The cognitive penetration objection

A different sort of objection against dogmatism involves appeal to cases of "cognitive penetration," cases in which propositional attitudes (beliefs, fears, desires, etc.) that the subject already has give rise to a related seeming. The cognitive penetration objection comes in two forms. The first is the "illegitimate boost" objection. If I have prior justification to believe that *P* (e.g., that my car is in my garage), and that belief causes me to have a seeming that *P* (e.g., the belief and expectation make it seem to me that my car is in my garage), dogmatism entails that the belief's justification goes up. The usual reply here is that the relevant claim is not counter-intuitive. I am not justified if I have a good reason to suspect that my having the seeming depends on my having the belief; but in the case where I have no such reason, it is not clearly counterintuitive to say that I am justified. Tucker (2013: 14) gives a useful analogy to testimony: if Bill and Jill both testify to me, at different times, that there is free pizza on the quad, then both testimonies give me more reason to believe than either of them separately, and this still holds if *unbeknownst to me* Jill knows only because she heard it from Bill.

The second form of the "cognitive penetration" objection is sometimes called the "tainted source" objection (Huemer 2013), and it arises from the fact that propositional attitudes other than justified belief—*un*justified beliefs, fears, desires, etc.—can influence how things seem to us. Suppose, for example, that Jill fears that Jack is angry with her, and that upon seeing Jack that fear causes her to have the seeming that Jack is angry with her (Siegel 2013). Many find it counterintuitive that Jill could acquire justification for the belief that Jack is angry with her in this way. The natural suggestion is that the etiology of the belief matters to its epistemic justification.[12] Once again, there are some who do not share the intuition that the subject's justification is affected by the belief's causal history when that causal history is not accessible to the subject (e.g., Huemer 2013). But at least some phenomenal conservatives admit to feeling the pull of the intuition in response to some of the cases, and attempt to account for it by saying that there is something else that is epistemically or intellectually bad or off in the situation—e.g., while the belief is epistemically justified, the agent is epistemically irresponsible, criticizable, or cognitively defective in some way (e.g., Skene 2013), or lacks the sort of justification that can turn true belief into knowledge (e.g. Tucker 2010). Some worry, however, that not all the problematic "tainted source" cases can be handled in these ways (e.g., Markie 2013 and McGrath 2013).

The problem of introspective beliefs

The phenomenal conservative faces an interesting problem in the case of simple introspective beliefs. I currently believe that I am experiencing a mild painful sensation (a headache), and my basis for this belief is just my experience of the pain itself. Now, in this case there is no intermediate "seeming to be in pain" state—I am and need only be aware of the pain itself in order to be justified in my belief. The belief is justified, no seemings required. How would the phenomenal conservative reply?

One possible reply, the reply that Huemer (2007) provides, is that it is compatible with phenomenal conservatism to claim that there is no intermediate state; there is just one state here: the state of seeming to be in pain and the state of pain are the very same, token-identical state. We have here a sort of self-referential state, a state that refers to itself or to part of its own character (the painfulness).

Perhaps we can push back on this response, however, if we keep in mind that seemings are supposed to be *propositional attitudes*. Even granting that one token state can be both a pain and a seeming to be in pain, the initial worry was not just that I don't need any intermediate state of seeming in order to be justified in believing that I am in pain, but that I don't need any *seeming that I am in pain*; I only need to have the pain and be conscious or aware of it, where, phenomenologically, this consciousness or awareness is not a propositional attitude. No doubt, the phenomenal conservatives will deny this—unless they want to allow that not all basic beliefs are justified by seemings.

A form of internalism?

Is phenomenal conservatism a form of internalism? More specifically, is it a form of access or awareness internalism? According to access internalism, in order to be justified in believing that P, I must be aware of or have some access to a reason in favor of P's truth. So, let us ask: if it seems to me that P, does that alone imply that I am aware of or have access to such a reason?

First, let's ask if its seeming to me that P involves any sort of access or awareness. Well, a seeming that P might involve a built-in awareness of its own content, the proposition that P; whenever it seems to me that P, I am aware of the content P. But awareness of a proposition alone cannot provide access to a reason to think that the proposition is true; if it did, then consciously thinking or believing that P would provide such a reason, and unless we are sympathetic to doxastic conservatism we should deny that it does. Perhaps a seeming that *P* involves an awareness not only of the proposition *P* but also of that forceful or assertive, strikes-me-as-true character that is distinctive of that attitude. Our seemings are rarely this reflective though, something that phenomenal conservatives have themselves usually pointed out. I have been experiencing various perceptual seemings in the last few minutes, and until now I was not aware of my having them. Still, perhaps seemings are *accessible*: while I can and typically do have a seeming that *P* without its seeming to me *that I have a seeming that P*, I am able quite readily to have the latter seeming. So perhaps, provided the phenomenal conservative thinks we do always have some minimal sort of access to our seemings, the phenomenal conservative can claim to satisfy the internal access requirement.

However, this will satisfy the internal access requirement as I have introduced it only if access to its seeming to me that *P* counts as access to *some reason or evidence in favor of P's truth*. Why should the fact that I am in this psychological state provide me with any reason to think that *P* is true? Indeed, as we saw in discussing the objection from evidential probability above, treating seemings as evidence seems to conflict with good probabilistic reasoning. Even if there's a way out of that specific problem without giving up access internalism, it makes intuitive sense to require that the subject be aware, somehow, of the relevance of the seeming to the truth or probability of the belief. But according to PC, I don't need any such reason to be justified. That is, it is not required that, in addition to its seeming to me that *P*, I have a reason to think that this seeming makes it probable that *P*. How, then, could the seeming that *P* make an epistemic, and not merely psychological, difference to one's perspective on the truth of *P*?

At this stage, the phenomenal conservative might choose to drop the internal access requirement or weaken it. They might claim that what is required is that one have access to some features relevant to justification (seemings), or drop the access requirement entirely. They might still accept a form of "mentalism" or "internal state internalism," the view that the justification of one's beliefs depends essentially only on mental states or what is in the mind. They will thereby preserve the intuition that subjects who are exactly alike internally have the same justification. However, a number of epistemologists, including some externalists we are about to consider in the next chapter, worry that the phenomenal conservative has sacrificed a very desirable feature of any account of epistemic justification: a robust connection between epistemic justification and the objective truth or probability of one's beliefs.

But we are getting ahead of ourselves. Let us turn now to a more careful discussion of access internalism and mentalism, and then to a discussion of reliabilism, arguably the most prominent externalist approach to the justification of perceptual beliefs.

1 Make a list of different examples in which one might naturally say, "it seems to me that *P*" or "it appears to me that *P*." In each case, what is the point of the expression? What are we trying to convey, or what do we mean?

2 According to phenomenal conservatism, perceptual seemings like the visual seeming that there is a book in your hands can be used to justify belief that there is a book in your hands. But then, you can infer from this that you are not merely dreaming that there is a book in your hand. Does that intuitively suffice to justify your belief that you are not dreaming? Now suppose that you actually begin to have dreams in which it seems to you that you are holding a book in your hand. Now, when it seems to you that you are holding a book in your hand, are you justified? You might think: "well, this is a book in my hand, so I am not merely dreaming, so this is not one of those times." Or does the fact that you have been dreaming provide a defeater? Suppose you think: "well, although I've dreamt this before, it seems to me that I am awake right now." Are you justified now?

3 Think of some specific, hypothetical cases in which the fact that you already believe that *P* causes it to seem to you that *P*, though you are not aware of this causal influence. Can the seeming still provide justification for that very belief (raising or boosting its justification to some degree)? What if that causal influence can be accessed, perhaps with some extended self-examination, though you are not aware of it at the moment. Would that make a difference to your justification?

Huemer provides a very accessible and extended defense of phenomenal conservatism in *Skepticism and the Veil of Perception* (2001). Pryor's work on dogmatism is more challenging, but rewarding; see "The Skeptic and the Dogmatist" (2000) and "What's Wrong with Moore's argument?" (2004). More recent defenses of phenomenal conservatism include Huemer's "Compassionate Phenomenal Conservatism" (2007) and "Phenomenal Conservatism Über Alles" (2013), Tucker's "Why Open-minded People Should Endorse Dogmatism" (2010), and Skene's "Seemings and the Possibility of Epistemic Justification" (2013).

Tucker's recent collection on *Seemings and Justification* (2013) is essential for serious research in this area. It includes discussions of the nature of seemings, the relation between phenomenal conservatism and internalism, and the problem of cognitive penetration, with a very helpful introduction surveying these and other topics. Some of the pieces below appear in the volume.

For more on the nature of seemings, see Sosa's discussion in *Virtue Epistemology* (2007: Ch. 3) for a version of the view that seemings are inclinations to believe. See also Tooley's critique in "Michael Huemer and the Principle of

Phenomenal Conservatism" (2013) in the Tucker volume. Most phenomenal conservatives hold that seemings are a special kind of propositional attitude distinct from doxastic states like belief and inclination to believe. For defenses of this view, see Huemer's work above (2001, 2007) and Cullison's "What are Seemings?" (2010). Granting that seemings are non-doxastic experiences of some sort, some recent work focuses on the relation between *sensation* and *seemings*. See the introduction of Tucker's volume for a brief discussion and some useful references.

For versions of the cognitive penetration objection, see Markie's "In Search of True Dogmatism" (2013) and Siegel's "The Epistemic Impact of the Etiology of Experience" (2013). For replies on behalf of phenomenal conservatism, see the pieces by Tucker (2010) and Huemer (2013) mentioned above.

See Cohen's "Basic Knowledge and the Problem of Easy Knowledge" (2002) and "Why Basic Knowledge is Easy Knowledge" (2005) for early presentations of the problem of easy knowledge; for some responses, see Pryor's "What's Wrong with Moore's Argument?" (2004) and Markie's "Easy Knowledge" (2005). For the related objection from probability, see the first piece by Cohen (2002) and White's "Problems for Dogmatism" (2006). For a useful survey of replies, see Tucker's introduction (2013: 18–20).

With regard to the relation between phenomenal conservatism and internalism, some discussion appears in Huemer's book (2001: esp. 20–2) but the topic is tackled more explicitly in "Phenomenal Conservatism and the Internalist Intuition" (2006), where he argues that phenomenal conservatism best captures the internalist intuition. For more recent discussions of this topic, see Tucker's introduction (2013: 22–4). See also Hasan's "Phenomenal Conservatism, Classical Foundationalism, and Internalist Justification" (2013), Bergmann's "Phenomenal Conservatism and the Dilemma for Internalism" (2013), Steup's "Does Phenomenal Conservatism Solve the Internalism's Dilemma?" (2013), and Huemer's "Phenomenal Conservatism Über Alles" (2013).

8

Access internalism, mentalism, and reliabilism

This chapter begins with a discussion of two prominent forms of internalism, access internalism and mentalism, and how they might be related. We see that in principle one could accept one of these without the other, and discuss which might be more fundamental. Some intuitive reasons are offered for taking access internalism to be more fundamental, or more central to the internalist-externalist controversy. We then distinguish between strong and weak versions of internalism. The rest of the chapter focuses on what is arguably the most prominent form of externalism—reliabilism—and objections to it. Reliabilism is motivated by the fact that it preserves the truth-conducivity of epistemic justification. We see that the problem of easy knowledge is also a problem for externalist versions of external world foundationalism like reliabilism, and briefly consider the question of whether it is a problem for all forms of foundationalism. We discuss some other problems as well: apparent counterexamples to the claim that external conditions are sufficient for justification (the Norman and Truetemp cases), apparent counterexamples to the claim that they are necessary for justification (the new evil demon problem), and worries to the effect that externalism's responses to skepticism are philosophically unsatisfying.

Varieties of internalism

While the roots of epistemological externalism arguably go further back, perhaps back to Thomas Reid (see the discussion of Reid in the second chapter), explicitly externalist accounts of epistemic justification have only been developed in the last forty or fifty years. The internalist-externalist controversy is difficult to characterize, and it may be that there are multiple controversies here, not a single one. But one of the main ways to draw the distinction is by asking whether a view requires that to have a justified belief the subject must have access to or awareness of some appropriate justifier or justifying factor—in particular, access to some reason or evidence in favor of the truth of the belief.

> **Awareness internalism or access internalism**: A subject S can be epistemically justified in believing that P only if S is aware of or has access to a reason in favor of the truth or probability of P.

An access-externalist or awareness-externalist is someone who denies the above requirement for epistemic justification.

> **Awareness externalism or access externalism**: A subject S can be epistemically justified in believing that P without being aware of or having access to a reason in favor of the truth or probability of P.

Given the way I have defined access internalism, awareness or access to reasons is a necessary condition for justification. Whether it is sufficient is left open. It is possible for someone to accept the access requirement while saying that justification also depends on some factors to which the subject does not have access. As paradigm externalists in the literature reject that access is a necessary condition for justification, it makes sense to understand the controversy in this way.

At the same time though, we should keep in mind that some who are access internalists in the above sense do accept "externalist" conditions— i.e., they do accept that one's justification depends in part on factors that are not or need not be accessible to the subject (Alston 1989; Steup 2004). In fact, even internalists arguably do, or should, take access internalism to be only a necessary condition, at least for *doxastic* justification. "*Doxastic* justification" for P is the condition of *having a justified belief that P*, while "*propositional* justification" for P requires only that one *have justification for believing P*. For an access internalist, propositional justification involves having access to good reasons for the truth of some proposition; doxastic justification requires not only having justification to believe that P (propositional justification), but also actually *believing* that P, and believing it *on the basis of* that justification. Thus, access to reasons in favor of one's beliefs may be sufficient (at least in the absence of defeaters) for *propositional* justification, but it is not sufficient for *doxastic* justification. Some access internalists might be tempted to require access to the fact that one believes that P on the basis of some good reason R in order for the belief that P to be doxastically justified. But this is implausible. If the majority of epistemologists are right in holding that the latter "basing relation" is causal in nature or involves a causal component, then we are rarely, if ever, aware of the basing relations between the beliefs we hold and the reasons we hold them on the basis of; even when it seems to us that we are so aware, we may go wrong about what the bases of our beliefs actually are. But, intuitively, we can be justified in believing something on the basis of good reasons, even if we mistake what our basis actually is. It is thus implausible to require access to the basing relation for doxastic justification. It is much more plausible to hold, as many traditional internalists do, implicitly if not explicitly, that access to reasons in favor of the truth of one's beliefs is necessary *and sufficient* (in the absence of defeaters) for *propositional* justification, but not sufficient for *doxastic* justification.

The internalist-externalist distinction is sometimes taken to turn on a different question: whether or not epistemic justification can be identified with or depends essentially and only on what is inside the mind, or on one's mental states.

> **Mentalism**: A subject S's epistemic justification for believing that P is identifiable with, or depends essentially and only on, S's mental states, or what goes on inside S's mind.

Let us include properties of mental states, and relations between mental states, among things that go on "inside the mind." Given mentalism, no two individuals can be mentally exactly alike and yet differ in the justification they have for their beliefs; any difference in justification requires a mental difference. Sometimes "mentalism" is taken to refer to this supervenience thesis. But let's distinguish it:

> **Mentalist Supervenience**: It is not possible for two individuals to be exactly alike mentally and yet differ in the epistemic justification they possess.

One who is an externalist in the sense of rejecting mentalism holds that one's justification involves or depends essentially, in part, on non-mental factors:

> **Non-mentalism**: A subject S's epistemic justification for believing that P can depend, in part, on factors external to S's mind or mental states.

How are these two forms of internalism—access internalism and mentalism—related? One might accept both forms, though perhaps take one to be more fundamental than the other. For example, one might take access internalism to be more fundamental. It is after all very intuitive that justification requires having a good reason or good evidence to think that a belief is true, and that having such a reason requires some sort of access to it. Suppose one also accepts the traditional view that one has access only to one's mental states (properties, internal relations, etc.). Would that be sufficient for mentalism? No—for one might take access to reasons to be necessary but not sufficient for (*prima facie*) justification, and take some external factors to be necessary as well. But suppose that one holds the stronger thesis that access to reasons in favor of one's belief is necessary *and sufficient* for justification.[1] One would then accept mentalism as well, as I've defined it.

One complication here is that, as we have seen, some (e.g., Johnston 2004) might hold that we can be directly aware of external objects, facts, or abstract entities, and take this awareness of extra-mental entities to make a difference to justification; *in a sense*, then, they would deny that justification depends *only* on the mental. But this depends on what we count as a mental state, or as part of one's internal or mental life. Those who accept that we can be directly aware of or acquainted with such external, concrete or abstract entities might take these entities to partly constitute experiences or mental states. It would therefore remain true for them that justification depends only on what is inside the mind. They can accept the mentalist supervenience thesis: there can be no difference in justification without a mental difference, assuming that *access to* or *awareness of* even a non-mental entity counts as a mental state. If I am aware of an external object or abstract entity, and you are not, but we are otherwise exactly alike, it makes sense to claim that we have different states of awareness, and so have different mental states. Thus, it seems that access internalists (who take access to reasons to be sufficient for propositional justification) would accept mentalism, or at least accept the mentalist supervenience claim.

Alternatively, one might take the mentalist thesis to be more fundamental, and argue that one has some minimal access to the relevant mental states that make a difference to justification, and so accept some form of access internalism as well. But what, exactly, is the motivation for mentalism itself, if the motivation is not access internalism? One thought is to take the supervenience claim to be fundamental and accept mentalism on its basis. Many do find supervenience of justification on the mental to be intuitive: if two individuals are exactly alike mentally, then they are exactly alike in terms of justification, no matter what the mind-independent world is like. For example, two individuals who are exactly alike mentally might be in very different circumstances—one in a world that corresponds more or less to common sense, the other in an evil demon world—but intuitively they have the same justification. (This is, as we shall see, one of the main problems raised against various versions of externalism.)

Some mentalists might even be inclined to deny access internalism, on the grounds that we often lack access to the relevant mental states or features that make a difference to justification.[2] If we are epistemically justified in our beliefs and supervenience holds, then our justification must depend on something mental; and if we don't have reliable access to the relevant mental states or properties, then epistemic justification does not require such access. One worry with the latter argument, however, is that it only works if we assume that we are epistemically justified despite lacking the relevant sort of access. Still, if the problem of access is serious enough, it may conflict with strong intuitions about particular cases of justification. This will be attractive to coherentists who want to deny access internalism (perhaps under the pressure of the problem of access we raised in the fifth chapter), claiming that justification depends only on what beliefs we have, and perhaps on certain relations between these beliefs, but deny that we have access to our beliefs or their coherence. Or perhaps some phenomenal conservatives will join in, denying that we need access to our seemings in order to be justified.

There is at least one other way to accept the supervenience claim and mentalism but deny access internalism, a way that doesn't depend merely on worries about access to the relevant mental states, but on what determines the contents of our mental states. Suppose one accepts the following view:

> **Content externalism:** the propositional or representational contents of at least some of our mental states depend essentially on what is outside the mind.

To get a sense of the view and the motivation for it, consider the following case, due to Putnam (1975).[3] Suppose that "Twin-Earth" is identical to our world in all respects, except that the clear, drinkable liquid in their oceans is composed of XYZ instead of H_2O. Twin-Earth people speak a language at least superficially just like English—Twinglish—such that they too, in similar circumstances, would express thoughts or beliefs such as that "water is wet," "snow is white," etc. Now consider two individuals, Oscar (an inhabitant of Earth) and Toscar (an inhabitant of Twin-Earth), who are identical in all internal physical respects—except of course that Oscar's body is made up of a lot of H_2O molecules while Toscar's is made up of a lot of XYZ molecules—and all mental respects that don't have to do with the contents of their thoughts. So they are disposed to behave, linguistically and otherwise, in the same ways. What should we say about the contents of the thoughts of Oscar and his counterpart on Twin-Earth? Suppose Oscar travels to Twin-Earth. He would initially believe that Twin-Earth has water in its oceans and lakes, that water falls from the sky in the form of rain and snow, and so on. But now imagine that he discovers that the water in the oceans and lakes here has an entirely different constitution—that it is XYZ, while water back home is H_2O. Calling back home, he might say, "Mom, you won't believe this: at first I thought that the transparent stuff in the lakes and oceans here is water, but I was wrong! They call it 'water', but it ain't water—it just *looks* like water!"

So Oscar's initial belief that "there is water in the oceans and lakes" is *false* on Twin-Earth, even though it is *true* on Earth. The opposite holds of the belief Toscar expresses by the same words or sounds. So they cannot be beliefs in the same proposition; they do not believe the same thing. Oscar's thoughts are about *water*, which is composed of H_2O; Toscar's thoughts are not about water but about something else—let's call it *twater*—which is composed of XYZ, not H_2O. And the contents of what they believe depend essentially on factors external to them, factors present in the external environments they were raised in.

While we have focused on the content of *beliefs*, there are many intentionalists about experience that hold that the contents of our *experiences* can depend in a similar way on the external world. For example, S and S^* might have color experiences that are internally indistinguishable, although S lives on Earth where "red" objects are red, while on S^*'s home world, "Inverted Earth," so-called "red" objects are green. Externalists about perceptual content claim that the experiential contents of our experiences depend on what color objects really have in our home environments. So, S^*'s experiences might be qualitatively indistinguishable from S's (or your or my) experiences of "red" but in fact represent green objects, because on his planet the indistinguishable experiences are normally produced by green objects.

Now we are in a position to see how someone might accept the supervenience claim, and mentalism, and deny access internalism. If one accepts externalism about the content of various beliefs and experiences, and accepts mentalism, one might agree with the mentalist that there is no difference in epistemic justification without a mental difference, but deny that it follows that we must have access to reasons in favor of the truth of our beliefs. Perhaps we can't tell "from the inside" what certain experiences or beliefs of ours represent, but those experiences and beliefs might still make a difference to justification.

Part of the point of discussing these admittedly controversial views in the present section—the view that we can have access to extra-mental entities, and content-externalism—is to show that the relationship between mentalism and access internalism is more complicated than it may initially seem.

However, I must admit that I suspect that the stronger underlying rationale is the access internalist one, and part of the reason for discussing externalism about content is to motivate the idea that access internalism is more fundamental. The access internalist will find the view that combines content-externalism and mentalism to be intuitively very problematic. What does it matter to justification whether something is mental or not, whether it is part of the content of our mental states or not, if we have no access to it? They might even appeal to Twin-Earth examples to make their case: while there may be good reasons to accept that this sort or dimension of content exists, or that our mental states have it, that would surely make no difference whatsoever to the justification subjects have for their beliefs. For example, differences between Oscar and Toscar's concept of "water" (prior to any discovery of H_2O and XYZ) make no intuitive difference to their justification. We can account for this intuition by claiming that only what one has access to can make a difference to justification, not whether something is internal to the mind.

I do not take this concern to be a conclusive argument for taking access internalism rather than mentalism as fundamental. It is open to the mentalist to deny that there is any such thing as external content or what philosophers of mind often call "wide" (inaccessible) as opposed to "narrow" (accessible) content. More plausibly perhaps, the mentalist might grant that there is some dimension of content that is fixed by external factors, but give some reason to deny that it is relevant—a reason other than that we don't have access to such contents. This helps bring out an important point: a better way to motivate mentalism is to defend a particular mentalist theory of epistemic justification, and so say more about *which* mental states or mental features are relevant to justification, something that the supervenience and mentalist theses don't do. Thus, for example, one might defend the phenomenal conservative claim that epistemic justification is purely a matter of how things *seem* or *appear* to the subject. Indeed, Huemer (2006) has argued that the core internalist thesis is just that there can be no difference in justification without a difference in how things seem or appear to the subject, and he denies access internalism. If one has concerns with the specific view of epistemic justification offered, however, then it won't provide a good motivation for mentalism.

The access internalist thesis, in contrast, is a highly intuitive thesis on its own, independent of a defense of any particular theory of justification. Many have appealed to the idea of epistemic responsibility as the underlying rationale for the access requirement. The idea is roughly that epistemic justification is a matter of epistemically responsible belief, and one can only be responsible for whether one believes on good grounds if one can tell or has some sort of access to what those grounds are. But the access internalist thesis is intuitive independently of that, and a number of internalists continue to accept it while denying that justification is a matter of epistemic responsibility. In any case, let us focus in the rest of this chapter on characterizations of the internalist-externalist debate that turn on the question that has, it seems to me, been traditionally more prominent, and the significance of which is intuitive on its face: does one have some sort of access to what is epistemically or evidentially relevant to what one believes—access to reasons or evidence in favor of the truth of what one believes?

Strong vs. weak access internalism

Access internalisms vary depending on what sort of "access" is required, and on what it is that must be accessed for justification. Let us briefly discuss the latter issue. According to the characterization of access internalism given above, S can be epistemically justified in believing that P only if S is aware of or has access to a reason in favor of the truth or probability of P. Notice that the latter doesn't tell us whether the subject must have access to the fact that the reason is a good reason for believing that P, access to the fact that it makes P probable. We can get stronger and weaker versions of internalism depending on whether we require access only to something, E, that is *in fact* evidentially or probabilistically relevant to P, or also require access to some evidential or probabilistic connection between E and P. This can apply both to foundational justification and inferential justification.

> **Strong internalism about foundational justification**: in order for S to be justified in believing that P, S must (i) have direct access to something, E, that makes probable P, and (ii) have direct access to a probabilistic or evidential connection between E and P.

In short, according to strong access internalism about foundational justification, one must not only be directly aware of something that is relevant to the truth of one's belief, but also be aware of its relevance. A weaker form of internalism might only require (i). Paradigm externalists deny both (i) and (ii). We can extend this to a parallel principle of inferential justification:

> **Strong principle of inferential justification**: in order for S to be justified in believing that P, by inference from or on the basis of the belief that E, S must (i) have justification for believing that E, and (ii) have justification for believing that E *makes probable P*.[4]

Most epistemologists accept the first clause. But virtually all externalists reject (ii): one can arrive at a justified belief in P by inferring it from E without being aware of or having justification for any sort of evidential or probabilistic connection between E and P. Phenomenal conservatives and dogmatists tend to agree with the paradigm externalist in rejecting the requirement that one grasp a connection between one's epistemic grounds or evidence and the proposition believed, at least for foundational beliefs (though they deny that external conditions like reliability discussed below are also needed for justification). Unlike these theorists, externalists typically allow that, at least in principle, one could have a foundational belief in the absence of any appearance or seeming.[5]

Reliabilism

While the externalist defends radically different views as compared with internalist foundationalists, the structure of knowledge and justification that emerges from such theories is still often a foundationalist one. We might first illustrate the point by examining the view defended by the most prominent of the externalists, Alvin Goldman's reliabilism.[6] The fundamental idea behind reliabilism is strikingly simple. Justified beliefs are reliably produced beliefs. Reliably produced beliefs are beliefs that are the product of a reliable process, and a reliable process is one that yields beliefs that are usually true (or would usually be true if enough of them were generated).[7]

Goldman initially distinguished two importantly different sorts of justified beliefs—those that result from belief-independent processes and those that result from belief-dependent processes. The former are processes that take as their "input" stimuli other than beliefs; the latter are beliefs produced by processes that take as their input at least some other beliefs. So, for example, it is possible that we have evolved in such a way that when prompted with certain sensory input we immediately and unreflectively reach conclusions about external objects. And we may live in a world in which beliefs about the external world produced in this way are usually true (or would usually be true if enough of them were generated). Such beliefs will be justified by virtue of being the product of reliable belief-independent processes. This is basically the "base clause" of the reliabilist's analysis, the principle of foundational or non-inferential justification: if a belief is the product of a reliable belief-independent process, then it is justified. Reliabilists generally add to this a condition requiring, in effect, that there be no defeaters available to the subject—e.g., no good reason or justification to think that the belief is false, unreliable, or untrustworthy.[8]

These foundational beliefs can in turn be taken as input for reliable belief-dependent processes in order to generate still more justified beliefs. A belief-dependent process is "conditionally" reliable if its output beliefs are usually (or would usually) be true if the relevant input beliefs are true. The output beliefs of conditionally reliable belief-dependent processes are justified provided that the input beliefs are justified. This is basically the "recursive clause" of the reliabilist's analysis, the principle of non-foundational or inferential justification: if a belief is the output of a conditionally reliable belief-dependent process, and the input beliefs are justified, then (absent defeaters) the output belief is justified.

The above is a crude sketch of Goldman's early reliabilism—he later modified it to deal with a number of objections. But the sketch is enough to bring out the foundationalist structure inherent in a reliabilist account. The reliabilist actually accepts the first clause of the principle of inferential justification introduced in the last section, but avoids the epistemic regress by embracing a kind of justified belief that does not owe its justification to other justified beliefs.

We have illustrated the way in which an externalist account of justified belief can exemplify a foundationalist structure by examining one of the most prominent versions of externalism, reliabilism. But other versions of externalism are also implicitly or explicitly committed to a version of foundationalism, or, at the very least, give an account that would enable one to distinguish non-inferential from inferential justification or knowledge.[9]

Externalist versions of foundationalism are probably attractive to many because they often allow at least the possibility of a much expanded foundational base of justified beliefs. Unlike Cartesian foundationalism, the reliabilist's distinction between non-inferentially and inferentially justified belief has nothing to do with whether the beliefs are somehow infallible or infallibly justified. If nature has been co-operative enough to ensure the evolution of cognitive agents who respond to their environmental stimuli with mostly true beliefs then there might be an enormous store of foundational knowledge upon which we can draw in arriving at inferentially justified conclusions. Moreover, many epistemologists hold that epistemically justified beliefs must in some way be truth-conducive or probable, and the requirement of reliability (or some other such external condition) makes the connection to the truth explicit, whereas other views that reject MSF like phenomenal conservatism threaten to sever the connection between justification and truth or probability.

Objections to reliabilism

Norman the clairvoyant and Truetemp

The very ease with which the externalist can potentially broaden the foundational base of non-inferentially justified belief is, ironically, one of the primary concerns with externalist epistemology. One of the most well-known objections to externalism attempts to show that the externalist's conditions for foundational belief are not sufficient for justification. Recall that for the reliabilist a belief is justified if it is the product of a reliable belief-independent process and there are no defeaters for the belief available to the subject. Consider BonJour's (1985: Ch. 3) famous hypothetical case of Norman: Norman is a highly reliable clairvoyant. His clairvoyance produces a belief that the President is in New York, but he has no reasons or evidence for or against the belief or its reliability. Intuitively, Norman's belief is unjustified. Or consider Lehrer's (1990) case of Truetemp, who, without knowing it, has a chip implanted in his head that produces precise and highly accurate beliefs about the ambient temperature. Intuitively, Truetemp's belief that the temperature is now exactly 47 degrees Fahrenheit is not justified.

There have been a number of attempts to respond to such cases. Some accept a modest form of internalism, introducing a relatively weak access requirement, e.g., that the subject must have an experience or accessible mental state that is a reliable way to arrive at beliefs, though the subject need not have access to the reliability of the experience (Alston 1989). However, there seem to be many possible cases, including versions of the cases of Norman and Truetemp, where these conditions are satisfied but the intuition is the same; we might suppose for example that the subject has, without knowing it, a highly reliable belief-forming process that takes some experience, like an itch, headache, or olfactory sensation, as input, and forms beliefs about the temperature, or the location of objects or people, but this intuitively makes no difference to the justification of the belief. (See Lyons 2009: 125.)

A different, more extended response is defended by Bergmann (2006: Chs. 1 and 2). Bergmann notes that proponents of the objection often claim that what the cases suggest is that there must be something one is aware of or has access to that makes a difference to one's perspective on the truth or appropriateness of the belief. Bergmann argues that this suggestion, as tempting or intuitive as it may be, leads to serious regress problems. For suppose that the internalist requires that one have access to something, X, that is in fact relevant to the justification of the belief that P, but that S is not aware of X's relevance to P. That is, suppose that S only accepts what I called weak (access) internalism. Then it is not clear why that should make any difference to the subject's perspective on the truth of P, any more than awareness of a reliable experience without any awareness of its reliability would make a difference to the subject's perspective. On the other hand, if we accept a strong condition to the effect that justification for a belief that P requires that the subject have access to something and believe that it is relevant to the truth or probability of P, that will lead to a problematic regress. For while this might make a difference to one's perspective on the truth, it only does so if S has justification for the belief that X *is relevant to the truth of P*. In order to have justification for that belief, the subject must be aware of something, X^*, and believe *that X^* is relevant to the truth of the proposition that (X is relevant to the truth P)*. But then, by the strong condition, one must also have justification for the latter belief, and so be aware of some X^{**}, and believe that *X^{**} is relevant to the truth of the proposition that (X* is relevant to the truth of the proposition that (X is relevant to the truth of the proposition that P))*. And so on. On this view, justification for any belief will require having justification for believing an infinite number of beliefs of ever-increasing complexity! That is not an ability that any of us have.

But the regress is not inevitable. If it is possible to be directly aware of or have direct access to some probabilistic or epistemic connections without that awareness taking the form of a justified belief that the connection holds, then the regress can be terminated. (This would also block clause (ii) of the strong principle of inferential justification discussed above from generating the same regress.) Bergmann claims that such a state of awareness, since it does not involve conceiving or believing of something as relevant to the truth or justification of a belief, can make no difference to the subject's perspective. But others deny this, holding that if it is granted, at least for sake of argument, that a direct awareness of relations of correspondence, entailment, or probability is possible, then it can make a difference to justification.[10] Consider the claim that we can have a direct awareness of logical relations of entailment and incompatibility without believing or judging that one proposition entails the other, or one property is incompatible with the other. For example, I have justification for believing that no triangles are circular, and justification for the inference from the belief that something is a triangle to its not being a circle. In these cases, it doesn't seem that I have, or need to have, a judgment to the effect that triangles are not circular in order to make the inference; I can grasp or be aware of the relevant incompatibility without judgment, and in such a way that it makes a difference to my perspective on the truth. So, if I see a green triangle, I can infer that it is a trilateral, that it is not red, that it is not a circle, and so on, and it is intuitive, even if controversial, to suggest that this is because I am aware of the relevant entailment between being triangular and being trilateral, or the relation of exclusion or incompatibility between being a triangle and being a circle, being green and being red, and so on. If, as some classical foundationalists insist, we can be directly, non-conceptually aware of such relations, it is not clear why that would make no difference to one's perspective on the truth of the relevant beliefs.

Others attempt to accommodate the intuitions in some way. Goldman (1986) argues that in the cases described it is natural to think that subjects like Norman do have defeaters available, and this explains our intuition to regard them as unjustified. However, many, including some other reliabilists, think it is easy to further specify or amend the cases to ensure that the defeaters are not available (Lyons 2009: 123–4).

A more recent attempt to respond to the Norman and Truetemp cases adds a restriction for basic or noninferential beliefs: they must be perceptual beliefs, beliefs produced by a "perceptual system"—very roughly, a system which constitutes a natural kind, whose lowest or most basic level inputs are energy transductions across sense organs, and whose inputs are not under the voluntary control of the subject.[11] Lyons (2009: Ch. 5) argues that the original Norman case doesn't specify whether the belief is a product of a perceptual system, and in the Truetemp case it is the product of an implanted chip and not a perceptual system; he also argues that once we change the details to make the beliefs the result of perceptual systems (e.g., imagining subjects who are normal members of an alien species that have perceptual organs for clairvoyance or precise temperature readings, and reliable processes of information transfer), the intuitions seem to change.

Just as the cases of Norman and Truetemp are designed to show that reliabilism makes getting foundational justification too easy, other, similar cases seem to show that reliabilism makes getting *non-foundational* justification too easy. Suppose, for example, that while you are asleep a group of logician-neuroscientists implant a device in your head that takes some of your highly reliable foundational beliefs (say, introspective or perceptual beliefs) as input and responds by selecting at random from a list of complex theorems of logic and producing a belief in that theorem. Intuitively, such beliefs are not justified despite their high degree of reliability. (This example is taken from Lyons 2009: 126.) One intuitive diagnosis is that the relation between the output beliefs and input beliefs is not evidential or inferential, or the process by which the output beliefs are generated is not an evidential or inferential one. The challenge for the reliabilist who wants to avoid saying that such beliefs are justified, and avoid adding internalist constraints, is to provide a better account of inferential processes, and one that does not require awareness of or access to a logical or probabilistic connection between propositions believed.

The new evil demon problem

The objections discussed above challenge the sufficiency of the externalist's proposed conditions for justification. The "new evil demon problem" challenges their necessity (Cohen and Lehrer 1983; Cohen 1984). Suppose that there is a subject that is just like you in all internal respects, except that while your beliefs are (let's assume) reliably produced, your twin's or counterpart's are not, for his or her beliefs are produced by a powerful deceiving demon. Intuitively, your twin is no less justified than you are. But given that your twin's beliefs are not reliable, the reliabilist must say that your twin's beliefs are not justified.

Various responses have been proposed. Some responses appeal to an ambiguity in "justification." For example, Goldman (1988) says that the counterpart's belief is "weakly justified" in the sense that the belief, though formed by an unreliable process, is one the subject is epistemically responsible or blameless for having, but the belief is not "strongly justified" in the sense that involves reliability. This does not seem to be adequate, for intuitively, there is something positive about the deceived counterpart's situation that is not captured by saying that she is epistemically responsible or blameless. A subject who reasons in accordance with principles that are defective in ways she cannot detect may have tried her best and be as epistemically blameless as an evil demon victim who attends carefully to her experiences and follows good principles of reasoning, but there's something clearly positive about the latter's epistemic situation that goes beyond epistemic blamelessness.[12]

Rather than simply deny the intuition, or explain it away by positing an ambiguity, a number of reliabilists attempt to accommodate the intuition by amending the conditions for justification. An earlier response by Goldman (1986) attempts to defend "normal worlds reliabilism" according to which a subject's belief is justified if the process producing the belief is reliable in normal worlds, where a "normal world" is, roughly, a world where our general beliefs about the actual world are true. It is no surprise that Goldman himself was quick to give this up. One obvious worry with this response is that it rules out even the *possibility* that "abnormal" processes like clairvoyance be justified. Another is that it rules out the possibility that our general beliefs about the world are unjustified (Pollock and Cruz 1999: 115).

More recently, some have suggested more sophisticated amendments to the conditions or to the sort of reliability required so as to accommodate the intuition while avoiding the problems of normal worlds reliabilism.[13] One such attempt is given by Comesaña (2002). For simplicity, let's focus on "foundational" or belief-independent processes, though the solution can be extended to conditionally reliable belief-dependent processes as well. Comesaña's "indexical reliabilist" solution claims, essentially, that the evil demon victim's beliefs can be regarded by the reliabilist as justified in the sense that *the belief is produced by a process that is actually reliable* or *reliable in the actual world*. The key to the solution is to take advantage of the indexicality of "actual," the fact that it refers to the world in which it is uttered, with the result that there are two different propositions associated with the claim that the process is actually reliable: (i) the "diagonal proposition," which says that the belief is produced by a process that is reliable in the world where it is believed, the world that is "actual" for the believing subject; and (ii) the "horizontal proposition," which says that the belief is produced by a process that is reliable in whichever world the proposition is considered, the world that is "actual" for those considering the subject. In order to count as *knowledge*, the process must be reliable in the former, the world of the believing subject, and so the demon victim's belief is not knowledge. But our beliefs as well as the demon victim's belief are *justified* in the sense that it is produced by a process that is reliable in the latter world, the world that is actual from the point of view of those considering the case (us). Thus, our beliefs (assuming we are not demon victims!) count as justified and as knowledge, while the beliefs of the demon victim count as justified, though not as knowledge. Moreover,

Comesaña claims that the solution does not posit two senses of "justification," but only one, and so is preferable to solutions like Goldman's (1986) that rely on a distinction between "weakly" and "strongly" justified belief.[14]

The problem of easy knowledge

The "problem of easy knowledge" already discussed in connection with phenomenal conservatism and dogmatism has been raised against externalism as well. For consider again the simple argument:

1   This table is red.

2   If this table is red then it is not a white table illuminated by red lights.

3   So, this table is not a white table illuminated by red lights.

Suppose that (1) is formed on the basis of a perceptual experience or a perceptual process in the absence of defeaters, and that beliefs formed in this way are highly reliable, so that, given reliabilism, (1) is foundationally justified. Suppose also that we accept the following intuitively plausible principle of closure: if S is justified in believing that P, knows that P entails Q, and infers on that basis that Q, then S is justified in believing that Q. It then follows that I am justified in believing (3). The problem is that it seems implausible that I could come to be justified in believing—let alone know—that the table is not a white table illuminated by red lights in this way. The objector takes the lesson here to be that (1) cannot be justified in the way that the reliabilist supposes. Justification can't be that easy. A few externalists deny the closure principle at work in the objection (Dretske 1970; Nozick 1981). But many externalists are reluctant to deny that it (or something like it) holds, for they do not want to deny that we could be justified in inferring (3) from (1).

Externalists also seem vulnerable to the second form of the problem of easy knowledge. They must apparently allow that a circular track-record argument could provide justification for belief in the reliability or trustworthiness of fundamental sources of belief. For example, the reliabilist can rely on perception to justify the reliability of perception, and memory to justify the reliability of memory. And it seems implausible that one could acquire justification for the reliability of such sources in this way.[15]

As already discussed in connection with phenomenal conservatism, some respond to both the deductive closure and circularity versions of the problem of easy knowledge by granting that such an inference is question-begging and epistemically ineffective if presented to someone who doubts the reliability or trustworthiness of such seemings, but deny that it follows that it can't provide a subject with justification at least when that doubt is absent (see Markie

2005; Bergmann 2008), while others respond that such arguments remain intuitively problematic, whether or not they are dialectically question-begging (Cohen 2005).

One might begin to wonder whether the problem of easy knowledge is a problem for *all* foundationalist views if it is a problem for any. It may seem that classical internalist foundationalists are in no better a position than phenomenal conservatives and externalists with respect to the problem, for they too will have to allow that one could rely on acquaintance with or direct awareness of facts to justify the existence and trustworthiness of acquaintance. Classical foundationalists might respond that the problem is not one of permitting circularity per se, but that when it comes to the sources and arguments they allow, the intuition that the knowledge or justification acquired is implausibly easy is absent or at least much weaker. To give a simple, intuitive example: I know that I am conscious, or have states of awareness, because I am aware of or conscious of them. I can also infer that I am not merely deceived into believing that I am conscious. While epistemologists may be suspicious of the notions of consciousness or awareness being appealed to here, the point is just that the intuition that this sort of knowledge is implausibly easy is missing. If the classical MSF view has a problem, the problem is that it makes epistemic justification of many of our beliefs very difficult to attain.

Unsatisfying responses to skepticism?

A general concern internalists have is that externalism provides rather unsatisfying responses to skepticism, responses that seem in a way not to take skepticism seriously. Many internalists are convinced that externalists are simply redefining epistemic terms in such a way that they lose the kind of meaning that they had at the beginning of inquiry, or that externalism fails to provide the kind of assurance of truth or satisfying response to skepticism that the philosopher seeks.

This concern is sometimes motivated by the problem of easy knowledge just discussed in the previous section. But another, perhaps more direct way of motivating this concern is by arguing that externalism provides at best a conditional answer to skepticism. According to externalism, *if* a belief satisfies certain external conditions (is reliably produced, caused by a fact that makes it true, etc.), then that belief is justified. This applies just as much to higher-level beliefs. According to reliabilism for example, *if* my belief that memory is reliable is itself produced by a reliable belief-independent process, then it is foundationally justified. If my belief that memory is reliable is the product of a track-record argument—presumably a conditionally reliable belief-dependent process—and *if* its input-beliefs are the product of reliable belief-independent processes then my belief that memory is reliable is inferentially justified. Either way, insofar as we are interested in a philosophically satisfying response to skepticism, the externalist seems to be giving a merely conditional response—assuming, having faith that, or hoping that the relevant beliefs are reliable. I might of course attempt to acquire scientific evidence for the reliability of some processes, but I would be relying on other (or perhaps the same) processes and so would be justified only *if* these processes are reliable. If I'm wondering whether or not I have justification to believe that God exists, I'm hardly going to think that my question has been answered when I'm told by the reliabilist that I might have a reliably produced belief that God exists or when I'm told by the causal theorist that my belief that God exists might be caused by the very fact that God exists. As far as satisfying intellectual curiosity, exemplifying reliably-produced belief or belief caused by the right fact is no more useful than having true belief. If I were to stipulate a technical sense of "foundational knowledge" according to which I foundationally know that *P* when I believe truly that *P* and my belief isn't caused by any other belief, there may well be all sorts of truths I "know", but will having such knowledge do me any good as far as putting me in a state that satisfies my intellectual curiosity?[16]

Bergmann (2008) carefully considers the charge that externalism is philosophically unsatisfying and argues that virtually all forms of internalism are vulnerable to the same concerns. They too provide at best the conditional response that *if* such and such internal conditions are satisfied (we have the relevant seemings or acts of awareness, and we lack defeaters) then our beliefs are justified. Also, as others argue (e.g., Sosa 1997 and Kornblith 2004), there is no reason why the externalist must deny that we can know or justifiably believe (in the externalist sense) the antecedents of these conditionals.

Perhaps the internalist's complaint is ultimately just that on the externalist's view there need not be anything available to the subject's perspective that is relevant to the reliability of her belief-producing mechanisms or processes in order for her to actually be justified in believing that they are reliable, and this seems counter-intuitive. If so, then the objection raised here is essentially the same one raised by the cases of Norman and Truetemp, though applied to higher-order beliefs. As we have already seen, Bergmann would argue that the advantage that the internalist claims to have here is illusory. If the form of access or awareness involves judging that something of which one is aware is relevant to the truth of one's belief, this leads to serious regress problems that make justification impossible. If on the other hand the internalist requires anything less than this, then the main motivation for internalism—that it makes a difference to the subject's perspective on the truth—is lost. However, as already discussed, a number of internalists deny that Bergmann's dilemma is successful.

1 Some philosophers motivate externalist views, like reliabilism, on the basis that they accommodate the idea that young children, and perhaps some animals, have knowledge regarding the external world via perception. How plausible are such arguments? Are they right that children and animals do have knowledge? Are they right that they fail to satisfy the internalist requirements?

2 Do you think Norman's beliefs that result from reliable belief-producing process of clairvoyance are justified, in the absence of defeaters? What if everyone happened to have reliable processes just like Norman's in society, and it is generally accepted that they are reliable, except that Norman has no awareness of this—would his beliefs be justified then? What if everyone happened to have reliable processes just like Norman's in society, but somehow neither Norman nor anyone else was aware of this, though they also had no defeaters—would any of these beliefs be justified?

3 Reliabilism, in its basic form, seems to imply that subjects in evil demon worlds who have perceptual experiences just like ours are not justified in these beliefs. Do you find this plausible? Is there a way that the reliabilist can explain away the intuitions of those who claim that demon victims are no less justified than we are (assuming we are not demon victims)—perhaps claiming that while these demon victims are not epistemically justified, they are blameless? Can you think of some ways for reliabilists to accommodate this intuition, perhaps by saying that there is a sense, perhaps an extended or weaker sense, in which the demon victims too have "reliable" beliefs?

For good introductory surveys on the internalist/externalist debate, see Poston's entry in the *Internet Encyclopedia of Philosophy*, and Pappas's entry in the *Stanford Encyclopedia of Philosophy* (2014).

For some influential defenses of forms of access or awareness internalism, see BonJour's *The Structure of Empirical Knowledge* (1985) and *Epistemic Justification* (in Sosa and BonJour 2003), Lehrer's *The Theory of Knowledge* (1990), and Fumerton's *Metaepistemology and Skepticism* (1995). For defenses of mentalism, see the work of Conee and Feldman, especially "Internalism Defended" (2001). For influential critiques of internalism, see Goldman's "Internalism Exposed" (1999) and Bergmann's *Justification without Awareness* (2006). For replies to Goldman, see BonJour's "The Indispensability of Internalism" (2001) and the Conee and Feldman article just mentioned (2001). For replies that focus on Bergmann's recent dilemma for internalism, see Matheson and Rogers's "Bergmann's Dilemma: Exit Strategies for Internalists" (2011), Hasan's "Classical Foundationalism and Bergmann's Dilemma for Internalism," and Fales's "Turtle Epistemology" (2014). For a collection of new, critical discussions of traditional forms of internalism, with some replies from Fumerton, see Coppenger and Bergmann's volume, *Intellectual Assurance* (2016).

Goldman's "What is Justified Belief?" (1979) is a classical piece on reliabilism. For a more recent version of reliabilism that focuses on perception, see Lyons's excellent book, *Perception and Basic Beliefs* (2009). For some other influential versions of externalism that we did not cover here, see Nozick's *Philosophical Explanations* (1981) for a "truth-tracking" account, and Plantinga's *Warrant and Proper Function* (1993) and Bergmann's *Justification without Awareness* (2006) for proper functionalism accounts.

On influential objections to externalism: For counterexamples to the sufficiency of externalist conditions (e.g., Norman and Truetemp cases), see BonJour's "Externalist Theories of Empirical Knowledge" (1980) or his book, *The Structure of Empirical Knowledge* (1985), and Lehrer's *The Theory of Knowledge* (1990). For some recent replies to such objections, see Lyons (2009) who argues that his conditions avoid the problem, and Bergmann (2006) who argues that the intuition behind these objections is too demanding and should be rejected.

The evil demon problem is presented by Lehrer and Cohen in "Justification, Truth, and Knowledge" (1983) and by Cohen in "Justification and Truth" (1984). For a useful survey of attempted responses, see LittleJohn's entry in the *Internet Encyclopedia of Philosophy*.

See Cohen's "Basic Knowledge and the Problem of Easy Knowledge" (2002) and "Why Basic Knowledge is Easy Knowledge" (2005) for early presentations of the problem of easy knowledge; for objections focusing on circularity in particular, see Vogel's "Epistemic Bootstrapping" (2008b). Fumerton's *Metaepistemology and Skepticism* (1995: Ch. 6) raises similar worries, and argues more generally that externalism fails to offer philosophically satisfying responses to skepticism; see also Stroud's "Understanding Justification in General" (1989). For a detailed reply to such concerns, see Bergmann on "Externalist Responses to Skepticism" (2008).

9

Epistemological disjunctivism

In this chapter we turn to recent defenses of epistemological disjunctivism, and in particular to Duncan Pritchard's (2012) defense of the view. We begin by distinguishing between metaphysical and epistemological disjunctivism, noting that they are logically independent, though some might find it natural to combine them. We then discuss the central motivation for epistemological disjunctivism, namely, that it provides the epistemological equivalent of the "holy grail," a view that makes it possible for the subject to have internal access to objectively truth-conducive (indeed, "factive" or truth-entailing) justification for one's perceptual beliefs. We then discuss some problems related to the view's access requirement, and an examination of the response to these problems raises the worry that the view is not well-motivated. We end with a brief discussion of whether epistemological disjunctivism does better against skepticism than the alternatives.

Metaphysical and epistemological disjunctivism

In the third chapter we discussed metaphysical disjunctivism, the view that the indistinguishable experiences in the "good" case (perception) and "bad" case (hallucination) are significantly different in kind: in the case of seeing a tomato, for example, one is directly aware of the tomato, whereas in the case of an indistinguishable hallucination, there is no such awareness.

One motivation for metaphysical disjunctivism is epistemological. If I am directly aware of some object's having some property F, then I am directly aware of the truth-maker of the proposition that the object is F. Much as classical, mental state foundationalists hold that being directly aware of certain mental states or facts involving them could provide reason or justification for belief about our own mental states, so too, a metaphysical disjunctivist might hold that being directly aware of facts involving external objects could provide reason or justification for belief about the external world. And they might deny that internally indistinguishable cases of hallucination could provide the same reasons, or reasons of the same kind—after all, in the hallucinatory case one is not directly aware of the truth-makers of one's belief about the external world. One could thus be moved to also accept *epistemological disjunctivism* and deny that internally indistinguishable cases of seeing and hallucinating are *epistemically* alike.

Just as some traditional views regarding the nature of perceptual experience might allow that internally indistinguishable experiences can be different in relatively minor ways, some traditional views regarding epistemic justification can allow that internally indistinguishable experiences can vary slightly in the degree of justification they provide. Even on a traditional mental state foundationalist view, internally indistinguishable experiences might involve awareness of slightly different qualities of experience or of sense data, and a difference in what one is aware of might make a difference to justification. However, the epistemological disjunctivist, like the metaphysical disjunctivist, makes a stronger claim. The epistemological disjunctivist claims that one's epistemic standing (degree of epistemic justification, or some other important epistemic property) is significantly higher in the case of seeing.

In principle, one might accept metaphysical disjunctivism but deny epistemological disjunctivism. For example, one might hold that, necessarily, if two subjects have internally indistinguishable experiences, then they must have equal justification. As metaphysical disjunctivists, they might hold that the character or content of our experiences are significantly different in the indistinguishable good and bad cases, but insist that this does not make a difference to one's epistemic standing.

One might also accept epistemological disjunctivism while denying or being uncommitted to metaphysical disjunctivism. One might hold that there is a significant epistemic difference between the internally indistinguishable good and bad cases, while denying or leaving open the possibility that the underlying experiences are significantly different. On this view, the difference in epistemic standing depends on the fact that one is a case of *seeing* while the other is not, but not or not necessarily because the *experiences themselves* are different. For example, one might hold that while the very same experiences are present in the good and the bad cases, they play a significantly different role due to other factors. These factors will have something to do with the experiences—for example, they will have to do with the relation between these experiences and the external world—but this is compatible with denying that the experiences themselves are the same. Thus, while the two views may naturally go together, they are logically independent.

Having made this observation though, we should guard against trivializing epistemological disjunctivism. There is, of course, a difference in *knowledge* between cases of believing based on seeing and cases of believing based on hallucinating, since in the latter case one's belief is not even true. Even in the case of veridical hallucination, one's belief doesn't count as knowledge because the belief is not related in the right way to the facts that make it true. So, in a sense, everyone or nearly everyone agrees that internally indistinguishable good and bad cases can be significantly different epistemically. But the epistemological disjunctivist's position goes beyond these relatively uncontroversial claims.

We can make the epistemological disjunctivist's claim less trivial or more substantive if we take it to be a claim about evidence, reasons, justification, or rational support. The claim might be, for example, that one can have evidence, reasons, justification, rational support (etc.) for one's belief in the good case but lack it in the internally indistinguishable bad case, despite their being internally indistinguishable; or that one can have evidence, reasons, justification, rational support (etc.) that is good enough for knowledge in the good case but lack it in the internally indistinguishable bad case.

Epistemological disjunctivism and the "holy grail"

Let's consider, for two reasons, the particular defense of epistemological disjunctivism offered recently by Pritchard. First, while certainly influenced by the epistemological disjunctivist views of McDowell (1995) and others, it is a relatively clear and accessible statement of the view. Second, although he admits that the view is highly controversial, and his own endorsement of it is rather tentative, he takes it to be worthy of serious consideration "because the view in question, if it were right, would represent the *holy grail* of epistemology" (2012: 1), at least of perceptual epistemology. It would secure goals that, as we have seen, are dear to many epistemologists, though most have given up hope of having them all:

1   Truth-conducivity or a truth-connection: A view of perceptual knowledge as involving belief whose rational or epistemic support has a strong connection to the truth.

2   Internal access: A view according to which the rational support we have in cases of perceptual knowledge is internally or reflectively accessible.

3   Anti-skepticism: A view that provides a more satisfying response to skepticism than the alternatives.

Not all epistemological disjunctivists accept these three conditions (e.g., Williamson's (2000) version of epistemological disjunctivism denies that one's evidence or rational support is reflectively accessible). But Pritchard sees epistemological disjunctivism as a way of accepting the insights of internalism and externalism while avoiding the difficulties with each.

Like externalism (and, perhaps, classical versions of foundationalism with arguably very skeptical implications), epistemological disjunctivism preserves a strong connection between justification or rational support and truth— indeed, the connection between perceptual justification and truth is even stronger than most forms of externalism: rational support is "factive" in the sense that it entails the truth of the proposition believed. While some have argued otherwise, Pritchard claims that seeing that P does not entail knowing that P. This is important, for Pritchard wants to argue that one could know that P *on the basis of* seeing that P. One reason for this is that I may have some good, though misleading, reasons to think that there in fact is no tomato on my counter (even though there is), or for thinking that there is a significant risk that I am hallucinating or being deceived somehow (even though I am not). Another is that, whether for good reasons or not, I might see that P without believing that P, for perhaps I believe, possibly irrationally, that I don't see that P. Thus, while seeing that P in a sense puts me in a good position to know that P, it doesn't entail that I do know that P. But if such defeaters are absent, and I believe that P on the basis of my seeing that P, then seeing that P can provide rational support for knowing that P. This attempt to defend the claim that seeing that P can be a basis for knowing that P is controversial, for while one can see an F without believing or knowing that it is F, many would deny that one can see *that P* without believing or even knowing *that P*. Still, let us assume, for sake of argument, that Pritchard's response to this "basing problem" is successful.[1]

The internalism can be developed in one of two ways: (i) by relying on metaphysical disjunctivism and the idea that genuine perception involves an experiential awareness of or acquaintance with the truth-making facts while hallucination does not; or (ii) by holding that in the case of a perception, one has access to the fact that one is having a perception, whereas in the case of a hallucination one does not have access to the fact that one is having a hallucination, or that one merely seems to perceive something.

Pritchard develops internalism in the second way (ii), which is not committed to metaphysical disjunctivism. More specifically, he suggests that a subject's epistemic support for believing that P is internally accessible if it is constituted solely by facts that S *can know by reflection alone* (2012: 13). Suppose that I see that there is a tomato on my counter. According to Pritchard's version of access internalism, if my rational support for the belief that P is that I see that P, then I can know by reflection alone that I see that *P*. So, in this case, I can know by reflection alone that I see that there is a tomato on the counter. There may be many facts about the situation that I do not know by reflection, such as that the visual process by which I form the belief is reliable. But epistemological disjunctivism does not take this fact to provide rational support for the belief; it is my *seeing* that there is a tomato on the counter that provides rational support, and that is something that, according to Pritchard's epistemological disjunctivism, I can know by reflection.

The motivation for epistemological disjunctivism

Pritchard offers three main motivations for epistemological disjunctivism (2015a: 592): First, there's the "naturalness of the idea of factive reasons in the perceptual case." Second, as just discussed, Pritchard claims that episte-mological disjunctivism "enables us to find a way past the long-standing *impasse* in the epistemic internalism/externalism dispute." And third, it offers an improved response to skepticism, one that avoids the radical skepticism afflicting internalist theories, while not merely sidestepping the problem of skepticism or changing the subject as externalist accounts do. Let us briefly discuss the first point, and then turn to worries related to the second and third motivations in the next two sections.

Pritchard is right that, in ordinary contexts, it's very often natural to defend or express one's reasons for perceptual belief by appeal to factive reasons. It's natural for me to express my reasons for believing that Lulu the cat is currently on the bed by saying that I *see* her on the bed; unless I have some reason to doubt this, it would be odd for me to express my reasons by saying I *seem* to see her on the bed.

As Pritchard is aware, though, the naturalness of such talk can also be explained by the fact that we ordinarily assume that our apparent perceptions are veridical. Moreover, disjunctivism seems to conflict with other ordinary intuitions and ways of speaking: if I am the victim of some illusion or hallu-cination, but I have no reasons to doubt the veridicality or reliability of my perceptions, then my experience still gives me a good reason for belief, even if it is not factive. Pritchard's response to such cases involves distinguishing *justification* and *blamelessness*. In such cases, the beliefs are *blameless* but *not justified*. However, as we discussed briefly in the previous chapter, this appeal to blamelessness is problematic, for intuitively, there is something positive about the person who is the victim of deception or hallucination that is not captured by saying that he is epistemically blameless. Subjects who form beliefs in seriously defective ways they cannot detect may have tried their best and be as epistemically blameless as an evil demon victim or brain in a vat who forms beliefs in line with hallucinatory experiences, but there's something clearly positive about the latter's epistemic situation that goes beyond epistemic blamelessness.[2]

Problems with access and indistinguishability

Since factivity is built into the epistemological disjunctivist's account, a likely worry is that the view is in conflict with intuitive internalist requirements on epistemic justification.

The new evil demon problem

The first problem is just a version of *the new evil demon problem* discussed in connection with externalism in the previous chapter. Consider the evil demon victim whose perceptual or sensory experiences are internally indistinguishable from those of the subject in the good case, enjoying (veridical) perceptions. Perhaps the subject in the good case and the bad case have the same mental states, or perhaps, in line with metaphysical disjunctivism, they have very different but internally indistinguishable mental states. Either way, the objection goes, subjects with internally indistinguishable states are intuitively alike in terms of the justification or rationality of their beliefs. But according to epistemological disjunctivism, this is not so, since the demon victim does not have factive perceptions.

Pritchard would question the rationale for accepting the thesis that subjects who are internally alike or who have internally indistinguishable states must be alike in terms of justification, or in terms of the rational or epistemic support they have for their beliefs. What is the motivation for this claim? It might be thought that the following thesis holds: the only facts that S can access by reflection alone are facts that a subject who is internally exactly alike, or whose states are internally indistinguishable to S, can access by reflection alone.[3] Since what one has access to is the same in the two cases, then, the justification must be the same. But the above thesis is something that the epistemological disjunctivist will deny. For example, the epistemological disjunctivist who accepts metaphysical disjunctivism denies that subjects in the indistinguishable good and bad case have access to the same facts, since the subject is aware of the truth-maker for the proposition believed in the good case, while the subject in the bad case is not, since there is no such fact. While Pritchard does not commit himself to that, he gives a parallel response: in the good case one can *know by reflection* that one *sees that P*; but in the bad case one cannot know that one *sees that P*.

The distinguishability problem

The second is what Pritchard calls the *distinguishability problem.* The problem is that everyone, including the epistemological disjunctivist, accepts that the good case of knowing that *P* by *seeing that P* and the bad case of *merely seeming to see that P* can be internally indistinguishable. According to Pritchard, if one knows that *P* in the good case, then one has reflective access to the fact that one sees that *P*. One can infer from that that one is in the good case, and not in the bad case. But then, it seems one can tell that one is in the good case, and distinguish it from the bad case, after all!

Pritchard responds to the problem by pointing out that in some cases we can know that we are in one sort of case rather than another even if we cannot discriminate between them *perceptually*. For example, I can know that the limes I see in the produce section of the grocery store are real and not plastic, even though I wouldn't be able to discriminate between them perceptually, at least not from a distance. Or take a famous example from Dretske (1970) that Pritchard uses for illustration: I can know that some animal I see at the zoo is a zebra rather than a cleverly disguised mule even though I would not be able to discriminate between them perceptually. The epistemological disjunctivist can use this distinction to argue that the subject can know she is in the good case even though there is a sense in which she cannot discriminate between the good and bad cases.

One might worry that in these cases, something other than the *seeing* is doing the epistemic work. For example, the reason one can know that what one sees is a real lime is that one has background knowledge that grocery stores don't stock their produce section with plastic limes; something similar can be said of the zebra case and others. That is why we can infer that we are in the good case. But according to epistemological disjunctivism, we can at least in some cases get some rational support and, in the absence of defeaters, knowledge, just from the perception that such-and-such is the case—for example, just from seeing *that there are limes*. And once again, the reflective access requirement yields that I can know in such a case that I see that there are limes, and so discriminate it from the case where I merely seem to see that there are limes. So it looks like the distinguishability problem remains. As I understand him, Pritchard would object that this argument fails to distinguish carefully between a kind of *perceptual*, or perhaps better, *merely introspective* distinguishability on the one hand, and *reflective* distinguishability on the other. Even if we focus on cases that don't involve additional background knowledge, the subject would have to be able to competently deduce from the knowledge that he or she sees that there are (real) limes to the conclusion that these are not merely artificial. This is compatible with holding that one could not tell the difference between the perceived qualities of real and plastic limes without resorting to such inferences from what one knows by reflection.[4]

The reflective access requirement is too demanding

The third and fourth worries I want to raise are related: they are both objections to the effect that the access requirement is too strong. First, there seem to be subjects who fail to satisfy it and yet can have rational support for their perceptual beliefs.[5] Suppose a child sees that *P* but does not have the capacity to know by reflection alone that she sees that *P*. Perhaps she does not yet have a robust grasp of the concept of *seeing*, or is unable to apply it well. Does that disqualify her perception or perceptual experience from providing rational support that *P*? Or suppose that I see that *P*, but I have a very strange, incorrect, view of how it is that I know that *P*—for example, perhaps I accept the Berkelean idealist view, except, unlike Berkeley, I deny that any of this counts as sensing or seeing; or perhaps I hold the view that God is responsible for producing images in my mind that correspond to the way my physical environment is, or that I have some telepathic ability to tell what objects exist, and would deny that I ever really see that *P*. Suppose these beliefs of mine are unjustified—I lack good reasons to accept them. But I accept them nonetheless. Do I still have the capacity to know by reflection alone that I see that *P*? If not, then must we deny that I have rational support for my perceptual beliefs? Must we deny that I know that I have hands?

These concerns are far from decisive. It is not implausible to suggest that very young children, those too young to be able to know by reflection that they see such-and-such, don't yet know. For the other sorts of cases mentioned, it is difficult not to suspect that, even if these subjects are sincere in their incorrect views about how we are connected to the world, they can know by reflection that they see such-and-such, and not merely in the sense that it is logically possible for them to know these things by reflection (that would be a very weak accessibility condition!). It is difficult to resist imagining such subjects to have or be able by reflection to have at least implicit knowledge that they see that *P*, and their having unjustified or irrational beliefs that conflict with this doesn't necessarily defeat the rational support they do have that they see that *P*.

The final concern, and the second to the effect that the reflective access requirement is too strong, is that it is in fact *impossible* to satisfy, for it leads to a regress problem that is similar to the sort we discussed for certain strong versions of access internalism in the previous chapter.[6] Suppose we accept as a general requirement that in order for one to have justification or rational support for P one must be able to know by reflection alone the facts that constitute one's justification or rational support for P. So, if one has justification for P, there must be some facts P^* that constitute one's justification for P, and one must be able by reflection alone to know that P^*. But then, in order to know that P^*, one must have some justification or rational support for it, constituted by some further fact P^{**}, and by the reflective access requirement one must be able by reflection alone to know that P^{**}. But then, in order to know P^{**}... Thus, in order to know anything, one must have the ability to know an infinite number of other things. Even if that were not a vicious regress in itself, that is arguably an ability we just don't have. Note that this problem does not depend on whether one's rational support must be *factive*; it depends only on the claim that we must know by reflection alone the facts that constitute that support.

A version of the access requirement that is put in terms of some sort of acquaintance or direct awareness, and not in terms of knowledge or justified belief, would be able to avoid this regress problem. In the context of defending epistemological disjunctivism however, that would seem to require a form of metaphysical disjunctivism. It requires accepting that there can be an awareness of external world objects that does not involve a mere representation of them, and taking this awareness to be relevant to justification. We already raised some concerns with that view in Chapter 3.

In response to this sort of concern, Pritchard claims that he proposed the reflective access requirement only in the context of an epistemology of perception, and not as a general requirement (2015b: 633–4). There is nothing incoherent about this response. But it does raise the concern that one thereby loses, or at least greatly weakens, what was supposed to be a major rationale for epistemological disjunctivism. If a central motivation was that epistemological disjunctivism secures the "holy grail" of internal access to reasons that are objectively truth-conducive, but then we are told that access to reasons is not a general requirement for knowledge or justification, then we are likely to be much less excited about the view, and wonder whether it really provides the "holy grail" we were looking for. For it is one thing to show how an access requirement can be satisfied in the case of perceptual knowledge, and leave open how it might be satisfied for other sorts of knowledge; it is quite another to concede that it cannot or should not be accepted as a general requirement. It might help to compare a classical, Cartesian foundationalism that requires that one's reasons or evidence, at the foundational level, be certain. Suppose the Cartesian foundationalist says that this view would represent the epistemological "holy grail": internal awareness of factive reasons. But suppose they then add: only paradigm introspective beliefs satisfy the internal access or internal awareness requirement. That would hardly warrant saying it represents the "holy grail." At best, then, the sense in which epistemological disjunctivism represents the epistemological "holy grail", if true, ends up being rather modest.

But perhaps some positive reason can be provided for thinking that the access requirement is appropriate in some cases, but not in others. That would be one way to motivate the view and explain why a constrained access requirement makes sense. It might help to ask, then, whether there is some further underlying rationale for the internal access requirement, and what that rationale might be. Pritchard follows a tradition that ties internalist access to epistemic responsibility.[7] Epistemic responsibility seems to require internal access: in order for me to be epistemically responsible for what I believe, I must have reflective access to the reasons or epistemic support I have for my beliefs (Pritchard 2012: 2). But if this is the underlying rationale, why should it not apply to all beliefs? Do only some beliefs need to be epistemically responsible, and others not? Or is it that epistemic responsibility doesn't always require this sort of reflective access? Pritchard seems to hold the latter. All knowledge requires a minimal kind of epistemic responsibility: "one's cognitive success should be significantly creditable to one's cognitive agency"; and this kind of epistemic responsibility doesn't always require reflectively accessible rational support (2015b: 634). But Pritchard claims that the agents often exercise a kind of epistemic responsibility that is more demanding, and that does involve reflectively accessible rational support. This doesn't yet tell us why the requirement is appropriate in some cases but not in others; it merely tells us that we sometimes satisfy a strong, demanding kind of epistemic responsibility, and at other times we do not. It thus seems that we still lack a clear reason to think that the requirement is appropriate in some cases but not in others.

The skeptical challenge

In the previous section, we saw that while epistemological disjunctivism might provide internal access to truth-conducive reasons for belief, this advantage is much more modest than the term "holy grail" would lead one to expect. What about the last of Pritchard's main motivations for epistemological disjunctivism? Is the view better able to respond to the problem of skepticism about the external world?

One of the main arguments for skepticism regarding the external world claims that whatever is accessible to the subject in the good case is accessible in the bad case as well. Whatever is accessible to the perceiver can be accessible to the dreamer or hallucinator; whatever is accessible to us in the real world can be accessible to the demon victim or the brain in a vat. But then, if what is accessible to us is the same in the two cases, how could we have good reasons to think we are in the good case rather than the bad case? Those who are willing to drop the requirement of access to reasons avoid this problem. They can deny that what justifies one in the two cases must be the same, since it is not constrained by what is accessible.

Given the above discussion of epistemological disjunctivism, it should be clear that epistemological disjunctivism too can deny that one's justification or rational support must be the same in the good and bad cases. In this respect it is like externalism. As we saw, it also denies that what we have access to in the good and bad cases are the same: in the good case, one has access to the fact that one is in the good case; in the bad case, one does not have access to the fact that one is in the bad case. Disjunctivism grants that the two cases can be internally indistinguishable, but as we discussed in relation to the distinguishability problem, it denies that this implies access to the same things.

There are three concerns with this sort of response to skepticism. First: As we have discussed in relation to epistemological methodology (see Chapter 6), it is not clear why one should take the fact that a theory would avoid skepticism, if true, is a good reason to accept the theory. It would be such a good reason if one had good grounds for thinking that skepticism is false, or for thinking that the commonsense perspective is true. But perhaps we do have such grounds. Or perhaps it is reasonable to assume a non-skeptical commonsense view as a point of departure, as a default but defeasible view. But this itself is a controversial matter that would require further argument.

Second: as we have seen, there is another response that other broadly internalist accounts offer, like the phenomenal conservative response that we can rely on perceptual seemings to justify our beliefs absent defeaters, and the abductivist view that the truth of our perceptual beliefs provides the best explanation for our sensory experiences. These views could be understood as granting that we can have access to the empirical and *a priori* reasons in the good and bad cases, but denying that because of this we lack good reasons to think we are in the good case. We have already discussed some concerns with these views. The present point is a modest one: if part of the motivation for epistemological disjunctivism is the objection that these and other views that take what one has access to in the good and bad cases to be the same, or that treat non-factive reasons as sources of justification, fail to provide good responses to skepticism, that motivation is only as strong as that objection, and the jury is still out on that objection.[8]

Finally: the view does not seem to do any better against the problem of easy knowledge that we discussed in relation to EWF versions of internalism and externalism. Insofar as the problem arises for those views, the same problem arises here. But perhaps the epistemological disjunctivist thinks the ease with which such responses work against the skeptic is a virtue, not a vice.

1 How plausible is it to accept metaphysical disjunctivism while denying epistemological disjunctivism? How plausible is it to accept epistemological disjunctivism while denying metaphysical disjunctivism?

2 What is it to "know something by reflection alone," and how could one know that one sees or perceives something by reflection alone? Consider some epistemological views we have discussed (coherentism; traditional, mental state foundationalism; phenomenal conservatism; reliabilism), and think about which of them could accept that we can know that we see something by reflection alone?

3 Suppose one thinks of epistemic justification as a matter of epistemically responsible believing: roughly, one is epistemically justified in believing something if one forms one's beliefs in a way that is responsible given the aim of truth and avoidance of falsity. Sometimes the internal access requirement is motivated by appeal to the idea that we can be held epistemically responsible for our beliefs only if we have access to reasons or grounds that make a difference to the truth or probability of our beliefs. Consider the subject with internally indistinguishable experiences to the perceiver, like the victim of evil demon deception. Is this subject being less responsible than the perceiver? If so, in what way? If not, then why shouldn't this subject too be epistemically justified?

Though a version of epistemological disjunctivism is defended by McDowell (e.g., see "Knowledge and the Internal" [1995]), we have focused on Pritchard's much clearer, though somewhat tentative, defense in his book *Epistemological Disjunctivism* (2012). For very useful reviews of Pritchard's book, see Smithies's "Review of Duncan Pritchard, Epistemological Disjunctivism," in *Notre Dame Philosophical Reviews* (2013), and Greco's "Pritchard's Epistemological Disjunctivism: How Right? How Radical? How Satisfying?" in *Philosophical Quarterly* (2014). For some critical essays by Littlejohn, Schönbaumsfeld, and Zalabardo, with some replies by Pritchard, see the book symposium in *Analysis* (2015).

For related readings focused more on metaphysical disjunctivism, see the suggestions at the end of Chapter 3.

Conclusion

Having reached the end of the book, it is time to step back and take stock. We began with an examination of Descartes' method of doubt, and the argument that we cannot secure knowledge of the physical world on the basis of the senses. The argument relied on the premise that there are no definitive or conclusive signs by which one can tell whether or not one is awake (or deceived in some way). In contemporary terms, the experiences we take to be veridical are phenomenologically or internally indistinguishable from experiences that are merely parts of a vivid dream or hallucination. Descartes' search for secure foundations of knowledge led him to look inwardly, to his own ideas and experiences, for here things are as they seem, and one can, at least sometimes, secure knowledge regarding the existence of oneself and one's own ideas, and use reason to bridge the epistemic gap between appearances and the external world.

As Hume made clear, however, the skeptical challenge is significant and not easy to avoid. There is no deductive route from our experiences to the physical world, and we have no direct way of examining the physical world to determine that some correlation exists between our ideas or sensations and the physical world. So, if we are to avoid skepticism, some other means of ascent to realism is needed.

We considered the attempt to bridge this epistemic gap between appearances and the external world by observing the order and coherence among our ideas. In the chapter on coherentism, we examined a version of this proposal, one according to which our beliefs are justified by their coherence with *other beliefs*. A significant worry is that coherentism cuts us off entirely from the input of the senses, so that there seems to be no good reason to think that coherence is likely to yield true beliefs regarding the external world. (One possibility is to insist that we have *a priori* reasons to think that coherent beliefs are likely to be true, perhaps because that would offer the best explanation for our coherence. However, that would seem to amount to giving up a pure coherentist view and hold that some beliefs are justified independently of their coherence with other beliefs.) Moreover, we saw that coherentism threatens not only to cut off our access to the way the external world is, but to make access to our own beliefs impossible! If we still hope to have robust access to reasons for thinking our beliefs are true, as Descartes insisted, then we must look elsewhere.

But perhaps we can salvage the attempt to bridge this epistemic gap between appearances and the external world by observing the order and coherence among our sensory experiences and apparent memories, which we can access more or less directly. While we found this Lockean abductivist strategy promising and worthy of further development, some quite significant challenges remain. First, what reason do we have to believe that our abductivist or explanationist reasoning is secure? We cannot rely on empirical knowledge to support it, for to do so would beg the question against the skeptic. But Humeans and those inclined toward empiricism will doubt that we can have purely *a priori* reasons for thinking that explanations that satisfy our criteria of coherence, simplicity, explanatory power, etc., are objectively likely to be true. Second, there is the concern that some skeptical hypotheses may turn out to be just as good as the real world hypothesis by these criteria. And third, it is not clear that we really do have introspective or internal access to the experiential data needed. We discussed some responses to these objections, but these were tentative and in need of further development.

Many contemporary epistemologists have turned to external world foundationalism, early versions of which are at least suggested by the writings of Locke and Reid, to sidestep the worries with the coherentist and abductivist alternatives. We examined the phenomenal conservative or dogmatist view that our beliefs can be justified, in the absence of defeaters, by perceptual *seemings* or *appearances*. One worry we discussed had to do with the nature of the latter states: if they are propositional attitudes like beliefs, or inclinations to believe, why should we take them to be good sources of justification, assuming we deny that the mere fact that one believes something is a good source of justification? Most phenomenal conservatives argue that these propositional attitudes are not any kind of inclination to believe, though we raised some worries with those arguments. Setting these concerns aside, we found that the account is intuitive from a commonsensical standpoint, and that it allows us to respond quite easily to skeptical concerns. But two concerns remained. First, many suspect that the account makes the acquisition of justification and the response to skepticism *too easy*, and we discussed a number of ways to motivate this worry, including the problem of easy knowledge and the cognitive penetration objection. Second, it remains unclear why its seeming to me that P provides me with any reason to think that P is true, so the view seems in tension with a traditional access internalist requirement and could sever the connection between epistemic justification and truth.

Some external world foundationalists deny or greatly weaken access internalist conditions, but accept another form of internalism, mentalism, according to which justification depends only on what is inside the mind. However, upon examining this view, and its relation to access internalism, we found it somewhat difficult to motivate independently of the internal access requirement. Moreover, the internal access requirement is intuitive on its own, as is reflected in the fact that the majority of epistemologists in the tradition, from Descartes onwards, have accepted the requirement in some form or other. While there are glimpses of externalism in the early modern tradition, they are often motivated by skeptical worries with access internalism, and a strong retreat from access internalism is a relatively recent development.

Many contemporary epistemologists doubt that we can get everything we want—accepting that epistemic justification requires internal access to reasons that are objectively truth-conducive, and avoid skepticism—and have decided to drop or weaken the access requirement in the hope of securing truth-conducivity and avoiding skeptical worries. Externalism is motivated by the fact that it preserves a strong connection between justified or appropriately formed beliefs and the truth, and that it avoids the apparently demanding internalist constraints, making it easier to allow ordinary adults, children, and perhaps even some animals to have perceptual knowledge. In the chapter on externalism we focused on reliabilist theories of justification and a number of common objections to them, including counterexamples to the claim that externalist conditions are *sufficient* for justification (e.g., Norman the clairvoyant, Truetemp), and that externalist conditions are *necessary* for justification (the "new evil demon problem"). Externalists have developed quite elaborate and sophisticated responses to accommodate these intuitions to some extent, and explain why the contrary intuitions that persist are confused or misleading. Many worry that these externalist responses miss the point, and that they merely sidestep the problems rather than responding to them in a philosophically satisfying way. One symptom of this, they say, is that despite avoiding the truth-conducivity worries with phenomenal conservatism, externalism makes responses to skepticism *too easy*. Does externalism address the concerns we initially had when we asked ourselves whether we do have knowledge or at least epistemically justified belief, or has it really just changed the subject?

We ended our examination of theories of perceptual justification with epistemological disjunctivism. The central motivation for epistemological disjunctivism (at least the version of it that we considered) is that it gives us everything we want, at least in the domain of perceptual belief: if true, it would provide what Pritchard calls the epistemological equivalent of the "holy grail," internal access to objectively truth-conducive (indeed, "factive" or truth-entailing) justification for one's perceptual beliefs. We noted that the internalism can be developed in one of two ways: (i) by relying on metaphysical disjunctivism and the idea that genuine perception involves a distinct, factive experiential awareness of the external world while the internally indistinguishable case of hallucination does not; or (ii) by holding that in the case of a perception, one is in a position to know by reflection alone that one is having the perception, even though in the indistinguishable case of a hallucination one is not in a position to know by reflection that one is having a hallucination. One very interesting feature of the view is that while it can agree that, in a sense, Descartes was right that the case of perceiving and merely dreaming or hallucinating are internally indistinguishable, that does not imply that what we are aware of or have reflective access to in the two cases cannot be different, even *significantly* different.

Epistemological disjunctivism is worthy of serious consideration in part because it accepts the internal access requirement as well as a robust truth-conducivity requirement. It is helpful to compare this with classical, Cartesian versions of foundationalism. They too accept a strong internal access requirement as well as a robust, truth-conducivity requirement. However, because of this, they face very serious skeptical problems for a wide variety of empirical beliefs, including perceptual beliefs. If the epistemological disjunctivist is right that we have access to reasons objectively connected to the truth of our perceptual beliefs, and not just to the truth of some of our introspective beliefs, that would be a significant improvement.

As we have seen, however, serious challenges remain for epistemological disjunctivism. One challenge we discussed is with the disjunctivist's internal access requirement. We can put the problem in the form of a dilemma: we can understand this access requirement either along the lines of (i) above, involving a state of acquaintance or direct awareness that involves the external world itself, or along the lines of (ii), involving the ability to know by reflection alone that one perceives the world. Route (i) involves a highly controversial metaphysical thesis with significant problems of its own (e.g., explaining why perceptions and hallucinations are indistinguishable, and doing so while avoiding problems like the causal argument and the "screening-off" problem). Route (ii) avoids these problems, but the internalist condition of being able to know by reflection alone what one's reasons are is a condition we often fail to satisfy (in cases that are intuitive cases of justified belief), and, more seriously, generates a regress if accepted as a general requirement. As we discussed, avoiding the latter problem by restricting the reflective access requirement raises questions about the motivation for the view: Why accept the requirement for paradigm or basic perceptual cases, but deny it elsewhere? And if we deny that it applies generally, do we really have the epistemological "holy grail" that we were looking for, or is this goal truly mythical? But perhaps epistemological disjunctivism can be developed in a way that provides more satisfactory answers to these questions.

If there is any conclusion to be drawn from our examination of these issues and related debates in epistemology and the philosophy of perception it is that while each of the main theories in the epistemology of perception has its own motivations and advantages, none of them is free of significant challenges and difficult objections. It is often tempting, in defending one's favored view, to emphasize its advantages and the disadvantages of its rivals, while ignoring or downplaying the problems with one's own view, or the benefits of the alternatives. It is important to guard against this temptation. Moreover, the more we understand about the motivations and arguments for competing views, the better our chances at developing more satisfactory responses to the central problems in the metaphysics and epistemology of perception. I hope that I have offered the reader some help along the way to this goal, some help in navigating through this difficult but fascinating terrain.

Notes

Chapter 1: Skepticism and foundationalism in early modern philosophy

1   All references to Descartes' work are taken from Cottingham, Stoothoff and Murdoch (1984 and 1985), henceforth 'CSM'. References in the text are to the volume and page number.

2   For a much earlier discussion of skepticism, see Sextus Empiricus' *Outlines of Skepticism* from the second or third century CE (Annas and Barnes 2000).

3   See, for example, Russell (1912: Ch. 2).

Chapter 2: Realism, idealism, and common sense

1   All references to Locke's work are to *An Essay Concerning Human Understanding*. References in the text refer to the book, chapter, and (where relevant) section numbers.

2   Some may worry that there is still something problematic about the skeptic's position. The skeptic might say to Locke: "I'm talking to you, but I don't know it," or "I'm talking to you, but I'm not justified in believing that I am." Such statements, sometimes called "concessive knowledge attributions," sound odd. But philosophers disagree about whether the oddity is a sign of something wrong *epistemically* or only *pragmatically*.

3   G. E. Moore (1959: Ch. IX) famously responds to skepticism by claiming that he has greater certainty that he knows such things as "here is a hand" and "this is a pencil" than he has in any of the premises of the skeptical argument for the conclusion that we have no such knowledge. Even if Moore is right about that, we are interested in why this is so—what is it about these beliefs that makes them count as knowledge?

4   References in the text are to Berkeley's *A Treatise Concerning the Principles of Human Knowledge* (1710), henceforth simply 'Principles', followed by the part and section; some are to Berkeley's *Three Dialogues between Hylas and Philonous* (1913), henceforth simply 'Dialogues'.

5   Berkeley may not really think that the possibility is genuine. He famously claimed that nothing can be like an idea but another idea.

6   We will discuss perspective and projective geometry again, in the sixth chapter, on abductivism.

7   See Berkeley's discussion of identity in the third of his *Three Dialogues between Hylas and Philonous*.

8   I owe this suggestion to Richard Fumerton.

9   Could acts of *seeming to perceive, seeming to remember, etc.*, also be a source of justification on Reid's view? Perhaps, but it is difficult to tell. Reid rarely discusses the skeptical cases such as those involving incorrect apparent perceptions or memories.

10 See Pust (2013) for a critique of Reid along these lines.

Chapter 3: Perceptual experience

1   See Barnes (1965) and Huemer (2011) for more detailed discussions of these sorts of problems.

2   See Chisholm (1942) on the speckled hen problem.

3   See, for example, Jackson (1977) and Robinson (1994).

4   See Huemer (2011) for some helpful discussions of epistemological objections to sense-datum theory.

5   See Ducasse (1942) and Chisholm (1957) for influential discussions of adverbialism.

6   I am not claiming here that the claim about awareness must be part of the adverbialist account of experience. The adverbialist need not accept that one is always or even usually aware of or conscious of qualities of experience. Most think we could become aware of such qualities, but that seems to be an independent issue for the adverbialist. However, if the adverbialist is attempting to account for the phenomenology or for how things seem, then there is pressure to add some kind of awareness or consciousness of these qualities.

7   See Siegel's "The Contents of Perception" in the *Stanford Encyclopedia of Philosophy* for more on the contents of perception.

8   See, for example, Reid (1764), Jackson (1977), Robinson (1994), and Travis (2004). For recent defenses of the claim that perceptual experiences have content, see Byrne (2009), Pautz (2010), and Siegel (2010a and 2010b).

9   There are a variety of kinds of intentional theories of perception, and at least three important questions that any intentional view must discuss: (1) What is the relationship between the intentional content of an experience on the one hand, and its phenomenal qualities (what it is like to have the experience) on the other? (2) Does the propositional content of a state depend essentially only on what goes on in the mind of the subject ("content internalism") or also on some external factors ("content

externalism")? (3) Is the representational content of sense experience conceptual or nonconceptual? While we do not discuss these issues in detail here, some related issues will come up elsewhere in the book as needed.

10 While Russell himself would sometimes use examples like the one in the text to explain his view, it is not clear that Russell really did think that the cat would ever be a constituent of the proposition believed. For Russell, ordinary names and definite descriptions ("the so-and-so") get analyzed away so that what is left is a quantified proposition (e.g., "there exists some x such that..."). Properties (universals) remain as constituents as well as whatever it is that the quantifiers are "picking out." But it is not clear that Russell would want whatever takes the value of the variable in the quantified statement to be among the constituents of the proposition. So, on Russell's own considered view matters are not as simple as the example used here might suggest.

11 My characterization of the Fregean view here draws heavily on Siegel's "The Contents of Perception" in the *Stanford Encyclopedia of Philosophy*. For a defense of a Fregean view of experiential content, see Burge (1991) and Silins (2011). For a critique, see Thau (2002: Ch. 2).

12 See Armstrong (1968: 218) for an argument along these lines. For interesting discussions, see Fales (1994) and Fantl and Howell (2003).

13 Martin (2004, 2006) defends negative disjunctivism. See Sturgeon (2006) and Siegel (2008) for worries with negative disjunctivism. For some replies, see Fish (2009).

14 See BonJour (2016) and Lyons (2009) for concerns about drawing epistemological objections from metaphysical theses.

Chapter 4: An introduction to contemporary epistemology

1 Some epistemologists attempt to solve the Gettier problem by doing exactly this, providing an "anti-luck epistemology" that is still compatible with a rejection of Cartesian infallibilism. Pritchard (2005, 2007) played a large role in advancing anti-luck epistemology. For a recent "anti-luck" attempt to respond to Gettier problems, see Hazlett (2015).

2 See Goldman (1976) for the first discussion of the barn façade case. The case was originally raised by Carl Ginet in a discussion with Goldman.

3 See BonJour (2010) for an accessible discussion of many of these problems and an argument that epistemologists should therefore focus on justification rather than knowledge. See Reed (2012) for a defense of fallibilism about knowledge and a response to some of these problems, including the Gettier problem and the lottery paradox.

4 David Lewis's "Elusive Knowledge" (1996) is a classical discussion of this problem and a "contextualist" solution. More recently, Dodd (2011)

develops the problem into a defense infallibilism. Stanley (2005 and 2008), Dougherty and Rysiew (2009), Fantl and McGrath (2009), and Brueckner and Bufford (2012) offer different responses on behalf of fallibilism about knowledge.

5   However, some prominent epistemologists have recently argued that knowledge should be central, and other epistemic notions like epistemic justification should be understood in terms of it rather than the other way round. See, for example, the highly influential work of Williamson (2000).

6   For a discussion of skepticism and charges of self-refutation or self-defeat, see Fumerton (1995: 43–53).

7   I owe this particular example to William Roche.

8   See BonJour (1985: Ch. 4) for an argument along these lines. For an earlier argument that was the inspiration for BonJour's, see Sellars (1963: Part I).

9   See Goldman (1979) for an early and highly influential "reliabilist" version of externalism.

10   However, Siegel's "Epistemic Charge" (2015) argues against this, claiming that perceptual experiences can be assessed epistemically.

11   See, for example, BonJour (1999, 2003).

12   Hume famously thought that necessary truths were made true by relations between ideas, and some other modern philosophers were sympathetic to that approach. On such views my belief that $2 + 2 = 4$ might be a belief about mental states/ideas—or at least a belief made true by relations between mental states.

13   For more on acquaintance and traditional foundationalism, see Hasan and Fumerton (2014).

14   See Davidson (1983) for a defense of this.

15   Some foundationalist accounts require, in addition to these conditions, that the subject have some sort of awareness of the relation of correspondence for foundational beliefs, and the inferential relations for non-foundational beliefs. We discuss these stronger versions of internalism in Chapter 8.

Chapter 5: Coherentism

1   See BonJour (1985) for a coherentist view of this sort.

2   For a similar characterization of coherence, see Ewing (1934).

3   C. I. Lewis (1946) suggests this understanding of coherence or, as he put it, "congruence."

4   For more on the development of more sophisticated conceptions of coherence and their problems, see Olson (2012).

5   One might worry that it's a short step from inconsistent justified beliefs to justified belief in a contradiction! To get the "lottery paradox" (and a similar "preface paradox" for the book example) one needs to add the claim that

justification is "closed under conjunction": if I am justified in believing *P* and I am justified in believing *Q*, then I am justified in believing *P and Q*. By repeated application of this principle, one could justifiably believe that *no ticket is a winner and that one ticket is a winner*! Many respond by rejecting the principle that justification is closed under conjunction.

6   See Kvanvig (2012) for a recent attempt at a solution.

7   As already mentioned earlier in the book, I am assuming a correspondence theory of truth. Some coherentists might attempt to avoid these problems by adopting a coherence theory of truth. Very few philosophers think that a coherence theory of truth is defensible, however.

8   Though see Poston (2014) for a defense of coherentism that says otherwise.

Chapter 6: Abductivism

1   The distinction between types and tokens is easily illustrated with examples. I have the same *type* of organs as you do, but not the same *token* organs; we have the same kind or type but not the same particular or token instance of that type—we do not literally share a particular heart. You probably have at least some of the same books in your home as I do in mine—same *type* of course, not same *token* (assuming we don't share the same home).

2   For a relatively accessible, not overly technical discussion of these issues, and an application to the problem of skepticism about the external world, see Huemer (2016).

3   See McGrew (1995) for a defense of simplicity along these lines.

4   See BonJour's (1999) related distinction between "analog" and "digital" explanations.

5   See Vogel (1990, 2008a) for one attempt to defend this claim.

6   See Pollock and Cruz (1999: 61–3).

7   See Pollock and Cruz (1999: 62) and BonJour (2007: Section III) for similar concerns.

8   Moser (1989) defends a view along these lines.

Chapter 7: Phenomenal conservatism

1   See Plantinga (1993) for an example along these lines.

2   For an attempt to respond to this and related objections, see McCain 2008.

3   Defenders of PC include Huemer (2001, 2007, 2013), Cullison (2010), Tucker (2010), and Skene (2013).

4   See Pryor (2000, 2004). It's worth noting that Jim Pryor, who popularized

this term, now uses it to refer to the view that "justification is sometimes both immediate and underminable" (2013: 96)—roughly, that justification can be foundational and yet can be defeated or undermined by other reasons. "Dogmatism" so understood is compatible with the rejection of principles PC and DOG.

5   For similar suggestions, see Tooley (2013) and Conee (2013).
6   See Cohen (2002) for an initial formulation of the problem.
7   See Vogel (2008a: 539–42) for other examples of this sort.
8   See Cohen (2005). For more rigorous presentations of the argument for this and other apparently counterintuitive implications, see White (2006) and Pryor (2013: Section 6).
9   See Tucker (2013) for a brief overview.
10 See Pryor (2013) for a discussion of this assumption.
11 See, for example, Weatherson (2007), Jehle and Weatherson (2012), and Pryor (2013).
12 See, e.g., Markie (2005, 2013), Goldman (2009), Lyons (2011), and Siegel (2013).

Chapter 8: Access internalism, mentalism, and reliabilism

1   As argued above, plausible forms of access internalism will accept this only for *propositional* justification.
2   See, for example, Conee and Feldman (2001, 2011).
3   See also Burge (1979).
4   For a detailed discussion of this principle, see Fumerton (1995).
5   Some epistemologists have combined some modest internalist requirements with externalist ones in their accounts of epistemic justification. See, for example, Alston (1989) and Steup (2004).
6   Most of what I say here is based on the early seminal paper "What is Justified Belief?" (1979). Goldman's view changed quite dramatically in his book *Epistemology and Cognition*, but shortly after publishing the book he returned to the earlier account for at least one conception of justification (strong justification). See Goldman (1988).
7   Defining the relevant notion of reliability is no easy matter. As these few remarks might indicate, reliabilists will inevitably move beyond actual frequencies and turn to propensities or counterfactuals in defining the concept of a reliable belief-producing process.
8   As Goldman (1979) recognized, specifying the needed condition in the base clause without using epistemic terms like "justification" and "reason" is a nontrivial matter.
9   See, for example, Armstrong's (1973) account of direct knowledge. Though

more complicated than a causal theory of knowledge, Nozick's (1981) "tracking" account of knowledge also allows a distinction between beliefs which non-inferentially track facts and beliefs which inferentially track facts.

10 For a reply along these lines, see Hasan (2011). For some other replies on behalf of internalism, see Matheson and Rogers (2009) and Fales (2014).

11 See Lyons (2009: Ch. 4) for more on what counts as a perceptual system. For our purposes, this rough sense of what belongs to a perceptual system will do.

12 See Pryor (2001: 117) for discussion of this point.

13 See Comesaña (2002), Majors and Sawyer (2005), and Henderson and Horgan (2006).

14 For a recent critique of this approach, though one that is concerned with formal issues in the philosophy of language, see Ball and Blome-Tillmann (2013).

15 See Vogel (2008b) for an argument against reliabilism along these lines.

16 See BonJour (2001), and Stroud (1989) for arguments of this sort.

Chapter 9: Epistemological disjunctivism

1 See Pritchard (2012: Part I, Section 5) for an examination of the basing problem for epistemological disjunctivism.

2 Smithies (2013) criticizes Pritchard along these lines. See Audi (1993: 28) and Pryor (2001: 117) for earlier discussions of this point.

3 See Pritchard (2012: 39ff.). Pritchard mentions only the possibility of internal physical duplicates, though it's clear that he would reject the same thesis applied to the case of subjects with internally indistinguishable states.

4 For a more detailed discussion of the distinguishability problem, see Pritchard (2012: Part 2).

5 See Conee and Feldman (2011: 290) for similar concerns.

6 For this sort of criticism of Pritchard, see Littlejohn (2015).

7 See, for example, BonJour's (1985: 8) discussion of responsibility and internalism.

8 Smithies (2013) makes a similar point.

References

Alston, W. (1989). *Epistemic Justification*. Cornell University Press.

Annas, J. and Barnes, J. (eds) (2000). *Sextus Empiricus: Outlines of Scepticism.* Cambridge University Press.

Armstrong, D. M. (1961). *Perception and the Physical World*. Humanities Press.

Armstrong, D. M. (1968). *A Materialist Theory of the Mind*. Routledge.

Audi, R. (1993). *The Structure of Justification*. Cambridge University Press.

Audi, R. (2001). *The Architecture of Reason: The Structure and Substance of Rationality*. Oxford University Press.

Audi, R. (2010). *Epistemology: A Contemporary Introduction to the Theory of Knowledge*. Routledge.

Ball, B. and Blome-Tillmann, M. (2013). "Indexical Reliabilism and the New Evil Demon." *Erkenntnis* 78 (6): 1317–36.

Bennett, J. (1965). "Substance, Reality, and Primary Qualities." *American Philosophical Quarterly* 2 (January): 1–17.

Bergmann, M. (2006). *Justification without Awareness: A Defense of Epistemic Externalism*. Oxford University Press.

Bergmann, M. (2008). "Externalist Responses to Skepticism." In J. Greco (ed.), *The Oxford Handbook of Skepticism*. Oxford University Press.

Berkeley, G. (1999 [1710/1713]). *Principles of Human Knowledge and Three Dialogues*. Oxford University Press.

BonJour, L. (1978). "Can Empirical Knowledge Have a Foundation?" *American Philosophical Quarterly* 15 (1): 1–14.

BonJour, L. (1980). "Externalist Theories of Empirical Knowledge." *Midwest Studies in Philosophy* 5 (1): 53–73.

BonJour, L. (1985). *The Structure of Empirical Knowledge*. Cambridge: Harvard University Press.

BonJour, L. (1989) "Replies and Clarifications." In John Bender (ed.), *The Current State of the Coherence Theory*. Kluwer.

BonJour, L. (1999). "Foundationalism and the External World." *Philosophical Perspectives* 13 (s13): 229–49.

BonJour, L. (2001). "The Indispensability of Internalism." *Philosophical Topics* 29 (1/2): 47–65.

BonJour, L. (2007). "Are Perceptual Beliefs Properly Foundational?" In Mark Timmons, John Greco, and Alfred R.Mele, (eds). *Rationality and the Good: Critical Essays on the Ethics and Epistemology of Robert Audi*. Oxford University Press.

BonJour, L. (2009). *Epistemology: Classic Problems and Contemporary Responses*. Rowman & Littlefield.

BonJour, L. (2010). "The Myth of Knowledge." *Philosophical Perspectives* 24 (1): 57–83.

BonJour, L. (2016). "Epistemological Problems of Perception." *The Stanford Encyclopedia of Philosophy* (Spring 2016 Edition), E. N. Zalta (ed.). Available online http://plato.stanford.edu/archives/spr2016/entries/perception-episprob/ (accessed June 8, 2016).

BonJour, L. and Sosa, E. (2003). *Epistemic Justification: Internalism vs. Externalism, Foundations vs. Virtues.* Blackwell Publishing.

Brueckner, A. and Buford, C. (2012). "A Tale of Two Fallibilists: On an Argument for Infallibilism." *Thought: A Journal of Philosophy* 1 (3): 195–9.

Burge, T. (1979). "Individualism and the Mental." *Midwest Studies in Philosophy* 4 (1): 73–122.

Burge, T. (1991). "Vision and Intentional Content." In E. LePore and R. van Gulick (eds), *John Searle and His Critics.* Blackwell Publishing.

Butchvarov, P. (1980). "Adverbial Theories of Consciousness." *Midwest Studies in Philosophy* 5 (3): 261–80.

Byrne, A. (2009). "Experience and Content." *Philosophical Quarterly* 59: 429–51.

Byrne, A. and Logue, H. (2008). "Either/Or." In A. Haddock and F. Macpherson (eds), *Disjunctivism: Perception, Action, Knowledge.* Oxford University Press.

Byrne, A. and Logue, H. (eds) (2009). *Disjunctivism: Contemporary Readings.* MIT Press.

Chisholm, R. (1942). "The Problem of the Speckled Hen." *Mind* 51 (204): 368–73.

Chisholm, R. (1957). *Perceiving: A Philosophical Study.* Cornell University Press.

Chisholm, R. (1980). "A Version of Foundationalism." *Midwest Studies in Philosophy* 5 (1): 543–64.

Chisholm, R. (1982). *The Foundations of Knowing.* University of Minnesota Press.

Chisholm, R. (1989). *Theory of Knowledge.* Prentice-Hall.

Christensen, D. (1994). "Conservatism in Epistemology." *Noûs* 28 (1): 69–89.

Coates, P. (2007). *The Metaphysics of Perception: Wilfrid Sellars, Critical Realism, and the Nature of Experience.* Routledge.

Cohen, S. (1984). "Justification and Truth." *Philosophical Studies* 46 (3): 279–95.

Cohen, S. (2002). "Basic Knowledge and the Problem of Easy Knowledge." *Philosophy and Phenomenological Research* 65 (2): 309–29.

Cohen, S. (2005). "Why Basic Knowledge is Easy Knowledge." *Philosophy and Phenomenological Research* 70 (2): 417–30.

Cohen, S. and Lehrer, K. (1983). "Justification, Truth, and Knowledge." *Synthese* 55 (2): 191–207.

Comesaña, J. (2002). "The Diagonal and the Demon." *Philosophical Studies* 110 (3): 249–66.

Conee, E. (2013). "Seeming Evidence." In Chris Tucker (ed.), *Seemings and Justification: New Essays on Dogmatism and Conservatism.* Oxford University Press.

Conee, E. and Feldman, R. (2001). "Internalism Defended." *American Philosophical Quarterly* 38 (1): 1–18.

Conee, E. and Feldman, R. (2004). *Evidentialism.* Oxford University Press.

Conee, E. and Feldman, R. (2011). "Replies." In Trent Dougherty (ed.), *Evidentialism and its Discontents.* Oxford University Press.

Coppenger, B. and Bergmann, M. (eds) (2016). *Intellectual Assurance: Essays on Traditional Epistemic Internalism.* Oxford University Press.

Cullison, A. (2010). "What are Seemings?" *Ratio* 23 (3): 260–74.

Davidson, D. (1983). "A Coherence Theory of Truth and Knowledge." In D. Henrich (ed.), *Kant Order Hegel*. Stuttgart: Klett-Cotta.

DePaul, M. (ed.) (2001). *Resurrecting Old-Fashioned Foundationalism*. Rowman & Littlefield.

Descartes, R. (1984–91). *The Philosophical Writings of Descartes*, v. I, II, trans. J. Cottingham, R. Stoothoff, and D. Murdoch, and v. III, trans. J. Cottingham, R. Stoothoff, and A. Kenny. Cambridge University Press.

Dodd, D. (2011). "Against Fallibilism." *Australasian Journal of Philosophy* 89 (4): 665–85.

Dougherty, T. and Rysiew, P. (2009). "Fallibilism, Epistemic Possibility, and Concessive Knowledge Attributions." *Philosophy and Phenomenological Research* 78 (1): 123–32.

Dretske, F. I. (1970). "Epistemic Operators." *The Journal of Philosophy*: 1007–23.

Ducasse, C. J. (1942). "Moore's 'Refutation of Idealism'." In Paul Arthur Schilpp (ed.), *The Philosophy of G. E. Moore*. Open Court.

Ewing, A. C. (1934). *Idealism: A Critical Survey*. Methuen.

Fales, E. (1996). *A Defense of the Given*. Rowman & Littlefield.

Fales, E. (2014). "Turtle Epistemology." *Philosophical Studies* 169 (2): 339–54.

Fantl, J. and Howell, R. J. (2003). "Sensations, Swatches, and Speckled Hens." *Pacific Philosophical Quarterly* 84 (4): 371–83.

Fantl, J. and McGrath, M. (2009). *Knowledge in an Uncertain World*. Oxford University Press.

Feldman, R. (2003). *Epistemology*. Englewood Cliffs, NJ: Prentice Hall.

Fish, W. (2009). *Perception, Hallucination, and Illusion*. Oxford University Press.

Fish, W. (2010). *Philosophy of Perception: A Contemporary Introduction*. Routledge.

Fish, W. "Disjunctivism." *Internet Encyclopedia of Philosophy*. Available online: http://www.iep.utm.edu/disjunct/ (accessed June 8, 2016).

Foley, R. (1979). "Justified Inconsistent Beliefs." *American Philosophical Quarterly* 16 (4): 247–57.

Foley, R. (1983). "Epistemic Conservatism." *Philosophical Studies* 43 (2): 165–82.

Forrest, P. (2005). "Universals as Sense-Data." *Philosophy and Phenomenological Research* 71 (3): 622–31.

Fumerton, R. (1995). *Metaepistemology and Skepticism*. Rowman and Littlefield.

Fumerton, R. (2006). *Epistemology*. Blackwell Publishing.

Gettier, E. (1963). "Is Justified True Belief Knowledge?" *Analysis* 23 (6): 121–3.

Goldman, A. (1976). "Discrimination and Perceptual Knowledge." *Journal of Philosophy* 73 (November): 771–91.

Goldman, A. (1979). "What is Justified Belief?" In George Pappas (ed.). *Justification and Knowledge* Reidel.

Goldman, A. (1986). *Epistemology and Cognition*. Harvard University Press.

Goldman, A. (1988). "Strong and Weak Justification." In James Tomberlin (ed.). *Philosophical Perspectives 2: Epistemology* Ridgeview Publishing Co., 51–69.

Goldman, A. (2009). "Internalism, Externalism, and the Architecture of Justification." *The Journal of Philosophy*: 106 (6): 309–38.

Greco, J. (2014). "Pritchard's Epistemological Disjunctivism: How Right? How Radical? How Satisfying?" *Philosophical Quarterly* 64 (254): 115–22.

Haddock, A. and Macpherson, F. (eds) (2008). *Disjunctivism: Perception, Action, Knowledge*. Oxford University Press.

Harman, G. (1990). "The Intrinsic Quality of Experience." *Philosophical Perspectives* 4: 31–52.

Hasan, A. (2011). "Classical Foundationalism and Bergmann's Dilemma for Internalism." *Journal of Philosophical Research* 36: 391–410.

Hasan, A. (2013). "Phenomenal Conservatism, Classical Foundationalism, and Internalist Justification." *Philosophical Studies* 162 (2): 119–41.

Hasan, A. and Fumerton, R. "Knowledge by Acquaintance vs. Description." *The Stanford Encyclopedia of Philosophy* (Spring 2014 Edition), E. N. Zalta (ed.). Available online: http://plato.stanford.edu/archives/spr2014/entries/knowledge-acquaindescrip/ (accessed June 8, 2016).

Hellie, B. (2007). "Factive Phenomenal Characters." *Philosophical Perspectives* 21 (1): 259–306.

Henderson, D. and Terence, H. (2006). "Transglobal Reliabilism." *Croatian Journal of Philosophy* 17: 171–95.

Huemer, M. (2001). *Skepticism and the Veil of Perception*. Lanham, MD: Rowman and Littlefield.

Huemer, M. (2006). "Phenomenal Conservatism and the Internalist Intuition." *American Philosophical Quarterly* 43 (2): 147–58.

Huemer, M. (2007). "Compassionate Phenomenal Conservatism." *Philosophy and Phenomenological Research* 74 (1): 30–55.

Huemer, M. (2011). "Sense-Data." *The Stanford Encyclopedia of Philosophy* (Spring 2011 Edition), E. N. Zalta (ed.). Available online: http://plato.stanford.edu/archives/spr2011/entries/sense-data/ (accessed June 8, 2016).

Huemer, M. (2013). "Phenomenal Conservatism Über Alles." In Chris Tucker (ed.), *Seemings and Justification: New Essays on Dogmatism and Phenomenal Conservatism*. Oxford University Press.

Huemer, M. (2016). "Serious Theories and Skeptical Theories: Why You Are Probably Not a Brain in a Vat." *Philosophical Studies*: 173 (4): 1031–1052.

Hume, D. ([1748] 1955). *An Inquiry Concerning Human Understanding: With a Supplement, an Abstract of a Treatise of Human Nature*. Bobbs-Merrill Educational Pub.

Jackson, F. (1975). "On the Adverbial Analysis of Visual Experience." *Metaphilosophy* 6 (April): 127–35.

Jackson, F. (1977). *Perception: A Representative Theory*. Cambridge University Press.

Jehle, D. and Weatherson, B. (2012). "Dogmatism, Probability, and Logical Uncertainty." In G. Restall and G. K. Russell (eds.), *New Waves in Philosophical Logic*. Palgrave Macmillan.

Johnston, M. (2004). "The Obscure Object of Visual Hallucination." *Philosophical Studies* 120 (1–3): 113–83.

Kornblith, H. (2004). "Does Reliabilism Make Knowledge Merely Conditional?" *Philosophical issues* 14 (1): 185–200.

Kvanvig, J. (2012). "Coherentism and Justified Inconsistent Beliefs: A Solution." *Southern Journal of Philosophy* 50 (1): 21–41.

Lehrer, K. (1990). *The Theory of Knowledge*. Routledge.

Lewis, C. I. (1946). *An Analysis of Knowledge and Valuation*. Open Court.

Lewis, D. (1996). "Elusive Knowledge." *Australasian Journal of Philosophy* 74 (4): 549–67.

Lipton, P. (2004). *Inference to the Best Explanation*. Routledge/Taylor and Francis Group.

Littlejohn, C. (2015). "Knowledge and Awareness." *Analysis* 75 (4): 596–603.

Littlejohn, C. "The New Evil Demon Problem." *Internet Encyclopedia of Philosophy*. Available online: http://www.iep.utm.edu/evil-new/ (accessed June 8, 2016).

Locke, J. ([1748] 2008). *An Essay Concerning Human Understanding*. Oxford University Press.

Lyons, J. (2009). *Perception and Basic Beliefs*. Oxford: Oxford University Press.

Lyons, J. (2011). "Circularity, Reliability, and the Cognitive Penetrability of Perception." *Philosophical Issues* 21 (1): 289–311.

Mackie, J. L. (1976). *Problems from Locke*. Clarendon Press.

Majors, B. and Sawyer, S. (2005). "The Epistemological Argument for Content Externalism." *Philosophical Perspectives* 19: 257–80.

Markie, P. (2005). "Easy Knowledge." *Philosophy and Phenomenological Research* 70 (2): 406–16.

Markie, P. (2013). "Searching for True Dogmatism." In C. Tucker (ed.), *Seemings and justification: New Essays on Dogmatism and Phenomenal Conservatism*. Oxford University Press.

Martin, M. G. F. (2004). "The Limits of Self-Awareness." *Philosophical Studies* 120 (1–3): 37–89.

Martin, M. G. F. (2006). "On Being Alienated." In T. S. Gendler and J. Hawthorne (eds), *Perceptual Experience*. Oxford University Press

McCain, K. (2008). "The Virtues of Epistemic Conservatism." *Synthese* 164 (2): 185–200.

McDowell, J. (1995). "Knowledge and the Internal." *Philosophy and Phenomenological Research* 55 (4): 877–93.

McGrath, M. (2013). "Phenomenal Conservatism and Cognitive Penetration: The Bad Basis Counterexamples." In Chris Tucker (ed.), *Seemings and Justification*.

McGrew, T. (1995). *The Foundations of Knowledge*. Lanham, MD: Littlefield Adams Books.

McGrew, T. (2003). "A Defense of Classical Foundationalism." In L. P. Pojman, (ed.), *The Theory of Knowledge: Classical and Contemporary Readings*. Wadsworth/Thomson Learning.

Moore, G. E. (1959). *Philosophical Papers*. Macmillan.

Moser, P. (1989). *Knowledge and Evidence*. Cambridge University Press.

Murphy, P. "Coherentism." *Internet Encyclopedia of Philosophy*. Available online: http://www.iep.utm.edu/coherent/ (accessed June 8, 2016).

Newman, L. "Descartes' Epistemology." *The Stanford Encyclopedia of Philosophy* (Winter 2014 Edition), E. N. Zalta (ed.). Available online: http://plato.stanford.edu/archives/win2014/entries/descartes-epistemology/ (accessed June 8, 2016).

Nichols, R. and Yaffe, G. "Thomas Reid." *The Stanford Encyclopedia of Philosophy* (Summer 2015 Edition), E. N. Zalta (ed.). Available online: http://plato.stanford.edu/archives/sum2015/entries/reid/ (accessed June 8, 2016).

Nozick, R. (1981). *Philosophical Explanations*. Harvard University Press.

Olsson, E. "Coherentist Theories of Epistemic Justification." *The Stanford Encyclopedia of Philosophy* (Spring 2014 Edition), E. N. Zalta (ed.). Available online: http://plato.stanford.edu/archives/spr2014/entries/justep-coherence/ (accessed June 8, 2016).

Pappas, G. "Internalist vs. Externalist Conceptions of Epistemic Justification." *The Stanford Encyclopedia of Philosophy* (Fall 2014 Edition), E. N. Zalta (ed.). Available online: http://plato.stanford.edu/archives/fall2014/entries/justep-intext/ (accessed June 8, 2016).

Pappas, G. (1971). *A Theory of Perception*. Princeton: Princeton University Press.

Pappas, G. and Swain, M. (eds) (1978). *Essays on Knowledge and Justification*. Cornell University Press.

Pautz, A. (2010). "Why Explain Visual Experience in Terms of Content?" In B. Nanay (ed.), *Perceiving the World*. Oxford University Press.

Plantinga, A. (1993). *Warrant and Proper Function*. Oxford University Press.

Pollock, J. (2001). "Nondoxastic Foundationalism." In M. De Paul (ed.), *Resurrecting Old-Fashioned Foundationalism*. Rowman & Littlefield.

Pollock, J. and Cruz, J. (1999). *Contemporary Theories of Knowledge*, 2nd edn. Rowman and Littlefield.

Poston, T. (2014). *Reason and Explanation: A Defense of Explanatory Coherentism*. Palgrave Macmillan.

Poston, T. "Internalism and Externalism in Epistemology." *Internet Encyclopedia of Philosophy*. Available online: http://www.iep.utm.edu/int-ext/ (accessed June 8, 2016).

Price, H. H. (1932). *Perception*. Methuen and Co.

Pritchard, D. (2012). *Epistemological Disjunctivism*. Oxford University Press.

Pritchard, D. (2015a). "Summary." *Analysis* 75 (4): 589–95.

Pritchard, D. (2015b). "Epistemological Disjunctivism: Responses to my Critics." *Analysis* 75 (4): 627–37.

Pryor, J. (2000). "The Skeptic and the Dogmatist." *Noûs* 34 (4): 517–49.

Pryor, J. (2001). "Highlights of Recent Epistemology." *The British Journal for the Philosophy of Science* 52 (1): 95–124.

Pryor, J. (2004). "What's Wrong with Moore's Argument?" *Philosophical Issues* 14 (1): 349–78.

Pryor, J. (2013). "Problems for Credulism." In C. Tucker (ed.), *Seemings and Justification: New Essays on Dogmatism and Phenomenal Conservatism*. Oxford University Press.

Pust, J. (2013). "Skepticism, Reason and Reidianism." In A. Casullo and J. Thurow (eds), *The A Priori in Philosophy*. Oxford University Press.

Putnam, H. (1975). "The Meaning of 'Meaning'." *Minnesota Studies in the Philosophy of Science* 7: 131–93.

Reed, B. (2012). "Fallibilism." *Philosophy Compass* 7 (9): 585–96.

Reid, T. (1997 [1764]). *An Inquiry into the Human Mind on the Principles of Common Sense*, D. Brookes (ed.). Pennsylvania State University Press.

Reid, T. (2002 [1785]). *Essays on the Intellectual Powers of Man*, D. Brookes (ed.). University Park: Pennsylvania State University Press

Robinson, H. (1994). *Perception*. Routledge.

Rogers, J. and Matheson, J. (2011). "Bergmann's Dilemma: Exit Strategies for Internalists." *Philosophical Studies* 152 (1): 55–80.

Russell, B. (1912). *The Problems of Philosophy*. Barnes & Noble Books.

Schönbaumsfeld, G. (2015). "Epistemological Disjunctivism by Duncan Pritchard." *Analysis* 75 (4): 604–15.

Sellars, W. (1963). *Science, Perception, and Reality*. Humanities Press.

Siegel, S. (2008). "The Epistemic Conception of Hallucination." In A. Haddock and F. Macpherson (eds), *Disjunctivism: Perception, Action and Knowledge*. Oxford University Press, 205–24.

Siegel, S. (2010a). "Do Experiences Have Contents?" In B. Nanay (ed.), *Perceiving the World*. New York: Oxford University Press, 333–68.

Siegel, S. (2010b). *The Contents of Visual Experience*. Oxford University Press.

Siegel, S. (2013). "The Epistemic Impact of the Etiology of Experience." *Philosophical Studies* 162 (3): 697–722.

Siegel, S. (2015). "Epistemic Charge." *Proceedings of the Aristotelian Society* 115: 277–306.

Siegel, S. "The Contents of Perception." *The Stanford Encyclopedia of Philosophy* (Spring 2016 Edition), E. N. Zalta (ed.). Available online: http://plato.stanford.edu/archives/spr2016/entries/perception-contents/ (accessed June 8, 2016).

Silins, N. (2011). "Seeing through the 'Veil of Perception'." *Mind* 120 (478): 329–67.

Skene, M. (2013). "Seemings and the Possibility of Epistemic Justification." *Philosophical Studies* 163 (2): 539–59.

Smithies, D. (2013). "Review of Duncan Pritchard, Epistemological Disjunctivism." *Notre Dame Philosophical Reviews*.

Sosa, E. (1997). "Reflective Knowledge in the Best Circles." *The Journal of Philosophy*: 94 (8): 410–30.

Stanley, J. (2005). "Fallibilism and Concessive Knowledge Attributions." *Analysis* 65 (286): 126–31.

Stanley, J. (2008). "Knowledge and Certainty." *Philosophical Issues* 18 (1): 35–57.

Steup, M. (2004). "Internalist Reliabilism." *Philosophical Issues* 14 (1): 403–25.

Stroud, B. (1989). "Understanding Human Knowledge in General." In M. Clay and K. Lehrer (eds), *Knowledge and Skepticism*. Westview Press.

Sturgeon, S. (2006). "Reflective Disjunctivism." *Aristotelian Society Supplementary Volume* 80 (1): 185–216.

Thau, M. (2002). *Consciousness and Cognition*. Oxford University Press.

Tooley, M. (2013). "Michael Huemer and the Principle of Phenomenal Conservatism." In Chris Tucker (ed.), *Seemings and Justification: New Essays on Dogmatism and Phenomenal Conservatism*. Oxford University Press.

Travis, C. S. (2004). "The Silence of the Senses." *Mind* 113 (449): 57–94.

Tucker, C. (2010). "Why Open-Minded People Should Endorse Dogmatism." *Philosophical Perspectives* 24 (1): 529–45.

Tucker, C. (2013). *Seemings and Justification: New Essays on Dogmatism and Phenomenal Conservatism*. Oxford University Press.

Van Fraassen, B. C. (1980). *The Scientific Image*. Oxford University Press.

Van Fraassen, B. C. (1989). *Laws and Symmetry*. Oxford University Press.

Vogel, J. (1990). "Cartesian Skepticism and Inference to the Best Explanation." *Journal of Philosophy* 87 (11): 658–66.

Vogel, J. (2008a). "Internalist Responses to Skepticism." In *The Oxford Handbook of Skepticism*, J. Greco (ed.). Oxford University Press.

Vogel, J. (2008b). "Epistemic Bootstrapping." *The Journal of Philosophy* 105 (9): 518–39.

Weatherson, B. (2007). "VII—The Bayesian and the Dogmatist." *Proceedings of the Aristotelian Society (Hardback)*. Vol. 107. No. 1, pt 2. Blackwell Publishing.

White, R. (2006). "Problems for Dogmatism." *Philosophical Studies* 131 (3): 525–57.

Williamson, T. (2000). *Knowledge and its Limits*. Oxford: Oxford University Press.

Zagzebski, L. (1994). "The Inescapability of Gettier Problems." *Philosophical Quarterly* 44 (174): 65–73.

Zalabardo, J. (2015). "Epistemic Disjunctivism and the Evidential Problem." *Analysis* 75 (4): 615–27.

Index

Lightning Source UK Ltd.
Milton Keynes UK
UKHW020351070622
404006UK00005B/657